# PROTECTING YOUR

# FAMILY

BY

# CHARLES F. STANLEY

THOMAS NELSON
*Since 1798*

PROTECTING YOUR FAMILY

Charles F. Stanley

Copyright © 1998, 2008 by Charles F. Stanley

Published in Nashville, Tennessee, by Thomas Nelson, Inc.

Editing, layout, and design by Gregory C. Benoit Publishing, Old Mystic, CT

ISBN 1-4185-2813-7

Printed in the United States of America

08 09 10 11 12 RRD 5 4 3 2 1

# Contents

# A Biblical Perspective on Your Family

All family problems ultimately have a spiritual root, and the Bible is the only book that gives God's wisdom on how to address spiritual matters. The Bible's advice regarding families is not theory—it is truth. Truth can and must be applied; it must be "lived out." The Bible tells us what is true and valuable, and it tells us *how* to live.

There are those who may say, "But today's world isn't like the time of the Bible. Families are different today." The truth is that the human heart has not and does not change. The God-ordained dynamic of family life has not and does not change. The tactics of the enemy of our souls have not and do not change. The Bible is our best source of wisdom on the human heart, human relationships, and spiritual strength and power. What the Bible has to say to you is as fresh and applicable to your life today as it has been to those in every century throughout history.

Furthermore, God's truth is not bound to any one cultural group, economic stratum, or race. The truths in God's Word are for all people. The power of God to *apply* those truths is provided by the Holy Spirit, who is given to all who have accepted Jesus Christ as Savior.

This book can be used by you alone or by several people in a small-group study. At various times, you will be asked to relate to the material in one of these four ways:

1. **What new insights have you gained?** Make notes about the insights that you have. You may want to record them in your Bible or in a separate journal. As you reflect back over your insights, you are likely to see how God has moved in your life.

2. *Have you ever had a similar experience?* Each of us approaches the Bible from a unique background—our own particular set of relationships and experiences. Our experiences do not make the Bible true—the Word of God is truth regardless of our opinion about it. It is important, however, to share our experiences in order to see how God's truth can be applied to human lives.

3. *How do you feel about the material presented?* Emotional responses do not give validity to the Scriptures, nor should we trust our emotions as a gauge for our faith. In small-group Bible study, however, it is good for participants to express their emotions. The Holy Spirit often communicates with us through this unspoken language.

4. *In what way do you feel challenged to respond or to act?* God's Word may cause you to feel inspired or challenged to change something in your life. Take the challenge seriously and find ways of acting upon it. If God reveals to you a particular need that He wants *you* to address, take that as "marching orders" from God. God is expecting you to *do* something with the challenge that He has just given you.

Start and conclude your Bible study sessions in prayer. Ask God to give you spiritual eyes to see and spiritual ears to hear. As you conclude your study, ask the Lord to seal what you have learned so that you will never forget it. Ask Him to help you grow into the fullness of the stature of Christ Jesus.

Again, I caution you to keep the Bible at the center of your study. A genuine Bible study stays focused on God's Word and promotes a growing faith and a closer walk with the Holy Spirit in *each* person who participates.

# The Challenge of Protecting Your Family

---

### ☙ In This Lesson ☚

*LEARNING:* WHY ARE FAMILIES IMPORTANT?

*GROWING:* WHERE DO THESE FAMILY PROBLEMS *COME* FROM, ANYWAY?

---

The family is under attack today. A divorce in our nation is occurring every twenty-seven seconds. We face a growing drug problem and a rise in pregnancies and AIDS among the teen population. Children run away from home at the rate of nearly 1.3 million a year. Many leaders give lip service to "family values" and the need to have strong families, yet the attack continues. To a great extent, the family is the number-one target of Satan.

Why is your family a target? Because your family is important to God. The family is the primary environment in which we learn spiritual lessons. The things that we hear taught at church—in Sunday school classes, sermons, Bible study groups—we are to *apply* at home. It is in the application of Bible-based principles that we truly learn how to live a godly life and how to do what is pleasing to the Lord. It is in applying God's wisdom that we grow in faith and in our desire for greater intimacy with our Creator. Perhaps nothing on this earth regarding you—apart from your own personal salvation—is as important to God as your family ties.

There is a second and more global reason that your family is important to God. If the family is weak, the church is weak. And if the church is weak, our nation becomes weak. There is no way that any person can be isolated unto himself. In the same way, no family can be isolated from the greater community—church, neighborhood, city, state, and nation. What happens to us in our families happens to others around us. Your family is part of God's greater plan for the extension of His kingdom throughout the earth.

## Recognizing the Source of Attack

Satan attacks the family in many ways: drugs and alcohol; rock music and its influence toward violence and suicide; peer pressure from ungodly children, teens, and young adults; excessive materialism; the breakdown of family togetherness; the cultural questioning of all values—each of these may be considered a source of "assault" against the family. Behind the obvious reality of these dangers, however, lies the silent, invisible, and insidious source of the attack: Satan. Regardless of what we are confronting in our families today, we must never lose sight of the fact that *Satan* is the source of all attacks against the family. He is the one who is plotting and scheming for the demise of *your* family, using whatever methods are available for the individual weaknesses of your family members. Never lose sight of your enemy as you seek to protect your family. Satan is the source of *all* evil.

It would be bad enough if Satan were attacking only the families of the unbelievers in our nation, but he has launched a major offensive against the homes of God's people. People who have been saved for years are finding themselves under attack. Couples who have been married 10, 20, 30, and more years are finding their marriages under attack.

What can we do to strengthen the home? Does the Bible have an answer for the protection and strengthening of family ties?

*First, we must recognize that this is a spiritual battle.* The weapons with which we defend our families against the assault of Satan are spiritual weapons. We must become experts in spiritual warfare, and we must be *experienced* in spiritual warfare. We must know what to do in prayer, and we must actually intercede for our families. We must fight the good fight, knowing with the confidence of a firm faith that we will win. As we act, Christ enables. As we engage in spiritual battle, Christ provides the victory.

*Second, we must engage in active, positive measures that will strengthen the family against attack.* Spiritual warfare is our ultimate defense against assault from Satan. But every person who has ever played any kind of sport knows that a good defense is not enough. One must also have a strong and positive offense. In the protection of our homes, that offense comes in the form of doing the "right things" to protect the family in a preventive, positive way.

## The Spiritual Purpose for Protecting the Family

This study booklet deals with both a good offense and a good defense for the protection of the family. Keep in mind always, however, that the ultimate protection for your family is a spiritual matter.

### ∽ The Goal ∽

Your goal in protecting the family is spiritual—that your sons and daughters might be active, positive, strong Christians in this life, and that in eternity you might stand with your sons and daughters before the throne of God and hear the Lord say to you as a family, "Well done, good and faithful servants." Nothing that you do as a parent is as important as helping your children secure their spiritual and eternal future.

## ⟨∞⟩ The Methods ⟨∞⟩

Your methods for protecting the family begin in the spirit realm. Family members become strong in Christ through the *teaching* and *applying* of spiritual principles within the home. It is in developing spiritual warfare skills that your family members are defended against spiritual attack. It is in offering praise and thanksgiving to God that the family is encouraged during difficult times. As much as you may desire to protect your family physically, materially, and financially, the foremost protection that you can supply to your family members is *spiritual* protection.

# God Will Help You!

Keep in mind continually as you engage in this study that what God *calls* us to do, God *equips* us to do. Many people feel inadequate and even fearful at the thought of engaging in spiritual battle for their family members. Others feel inept and overwhelmed at the thought of being responsible for the spiritual education and enrichment of their children. Certainly, parenting is not for the faint of heart! Even so, what God has challenged us to do, He also will enable us to do by the power of His Holy Spirit.

You must be obedient to the Lord, and you must trust God to do what only God can do. Only God can redeem, save, and fill your children with His Holy Spirit. Only God can deliver from the enemy. Only God can heal, reconcile, and make whole. We do everything that we know to do, and then we must use our faith to believe that God will be faithful to His Word and work all things together for our good and the good of those whom we love (Rom. 8:28).

Protecting your family is a matter of entrusting your family completely to God. God loves you and your family members even more than you do! His love is never-ending, His power is beyond measure, His wisdom is infinite. And He *will* respond to your faithful obedience.

❧ What areas of your family life today do you feel need to be strengthened?

❧ What specific needs in your family life do you hope to address in this study?

❧ How do you feel about your role in protecting your family against the spiritual attacks of Satan?

---

### ❧ Today and Tomorrow ❧

*TODAY:* GOD SETS A VERY HIGH VALUE UPON THE SPIRITUAL HEALTH OF MY FAMILY, AND I AM ACCOUNTABLE TO HIM FOR THE SPIRITUAL WELFARE OF MY SPOUSE AND CHILDREN.

*TOMORROW:* I WILL BEGIN THIS WEEK TO PRAY FAITHFULLY FOR MY WHOLE FAMILY.

## LESSON 2

# Foundation Principles for a Godly Home

---— ❧ **In This Lesson** ❧ ——---

*LEARNING:* WHY ARE DIVISION AND DISAGREEMENT SUCH BIG PROBLEMS TODAY?

*GROWING:* HOW CAN I HOPE TO OVERCOME DIVISION WITHIN MY FAMILY?

---

The attack against the home is a spiritual attack, and the key question that we must ask ourselves as parents, grandparents, aunts, and uncles is this: "How can I develop a strong *spiritual* foundation for a godly family?"

In the Gospel of Matthew, Jesus taught about the "strong man" who comes to attack a house. In this parable, we find two important principles for establishing a godly home—indisputable principles upon which you can stake your family life. Just prior to this teaching, Jesus had healed a man who was demon-possessed, blind, and mute. The man was delivered from Satan's power, and immediately he could both speak and see. The amazed multitudes began to ask, "Could this be the Son of David?"

To squelch any thought that Jesus might be the Messiah, a group of Pharisees accused Jesus of casting out demons by the power of Beelzebub, the ruler of the demons. Here is what Jesus said in reply to their accusation (Matthew 12:25–29):

Jesus knew their thoughts, and said to them: "Every kingdom divided against itself is brought to desolation, and every city or house divided against itself will not stand. If Satan casts out Satan, he is divided against himself. How then will his kingdom stand? And if I cast out demons by Beelzebub, by whom do your sons cast them out? Therefore they shall be your judges. But if I cast out demons by the Spirit of God, surely the kingdom of God has come upon you. Or how can one enter a strong man's house and plunder his goods, unless he first binds the strong man? And then he will plunder his house.

Jesus made these two points very clear in His response to the Pharisees:

1. Division brings desolation.

2. God is greater than any satanic power.

## Division Brings Desolation

First, Jesus said, "Every kingdom divided against itself is brought to desolation, and every city or house divided against itself will not stand" (Matt. 12:25). We see that principle at work all around us. If a church becomes divided—some of the people holding one opinion, some another—the church will become splintered or "split," and if that breach continues, the church may eventually disintegrate and disband. The division initially may not be over anything that is all that earthshaking. It's not the *reason* for the division that brings about the desolation; rather, it is the fact that the people have allowed themselves to become divided.

9

The same thing happens in the home. If a husband and wife or a parent and child become divided, the home as a whole will feel that division, and it will be fractured and weakened. The family may eventually experience a "split," even to the point of separation, estrangement and alienation, and perhaps divorce or the "disowning" of a child by a parent or a parent by a child. The most potent means of destroying any institution is *internal strife* or internal conflict. An undivided, unified family or church can withstand virtually any external onslaught. But an internal conflict brings about distrust, division, and disintegration.

Jesus said, "If Satan casts out Satan, he is divided against himself. How then will his kingdom stand?" (Matt. 12:26). In other words, Jesus argued, "If you are accusing me of doing miracles by Satan, then Satan is actually working against himself—he is put into a position of both healing and destroying. That simply isn't possible."

✍ When have you witnessed a division in church, family, or work that brought about a feeling of desolation or destruction?

For you are all sons of God through faith in Christ Jesus. For as many of you as were baptized into Christ have put on Christ. There is neither Jew nor Greek, there is neither slave nor free, there is neither male nor female; for you are all one in Christ Jesus.

—Galatians 3:26-28

๑ What does it mean to "put on Christ"? If we are all "clothed in Christ," what does that suggest about division and in-fighting?

## Inner Division

Division usually begins as an "inner conflict" or a "divided mind." A person begins to hold an opinion that is *contrary* to God's absolute commandments or desires. The exact opposite of this state is to be "one in the Spirit," to hold fast to the central truth of God's Word and to what God wants us to do, say, and be. The godhead—Father, Son, and Holy Spirit—is our great example of unity. Jesus never did anything that He had not "seen" His Father do first. The Spirit flows from the Father and the Son in complete harmony. In like manner, we are called to discern the will of God and then to do it. As we come to a full understanding of God's will, we *can* experience unity in the Spirit. We will still have differences of personality and style, but our choices and behavior are to be rooted in God's absolutes.

11

Only let your conduct be worthy of the gospel of Christ, so that ... you stand fast in one spirit, with one mind striving together for the faith of the gospel.

—Philippians 1:27

⚘ What sorts of conduct are "worthy of the gospel of Christ"? What sorts are *not*?

⚘ What sort of "striving" is Paul recommending to us in this verse? Against what are we "striving"?

## ∽ Satan Cannot Produce Good ∽

Throughout the Scriptures, "division" among God's people is associated with negative situations and outcomes. Israel collapsed as a nation when it became divided, the northern tribes warring against the southern tribes. The Israelites later rebelled against God and became divided, attempting to serve both God and false gods—and great calamity befell them. Paul and Peter's teaching about submission is rooted in the understanding that unity and harmony are to prevail over division and disharmony.

In confronting the Pharisees, Jesus was saying that division brings desolation, and that Satan simply isn't capable of bringing about any-thing *good*. Satan's purpose for the family is always to bring about its destruction. Nothing that he does with regard to the family is for the good of the family, although many of the things that he uses as tempta-tions may *seem* to be for the family's good.

For example, Satan is tempting many families these days by saying, "It's important that parents spend time with their children. Since time is of such great value, it's more important that parents spend time with their children on Sunday mornings and Sunday evenings than to bring their children to church." Satan's temptation is that parents spend time with their children at home rather than at church, thinking that the net result will be of a greater good to the family. Not so! It is the family that prays together and worships together that stays united in faith—not the family that watches cartoons together or plays tennis together on Sunday mornings. Giving into a temptation to stay away from church brings about a "division" between a family and the church as a whole.

As another example, Satan may tempt a father by saying, "You could do so much more for your children and for your family as a whole if you just used the money that you now give to the church for your chil-dren instead." Not so! Giving to God what rightfully belongs to God sends a message to children of obedience, discipline, and God-centered priorities. Those values are weakened greatly when a parent says to a child, "Your pair of designer jeans is more important than giving to the church," or "Buying you a new car is more valuable than giving to mis-sions." The end result of such thinking is a divided mind about material and financial priorities.

The temptations of Satan often appear good in principle, but under-neath they are deadly and divisive to one's faith.

Beloved, do not believe every spirit, but test the spirits, whether they are of God; because many false prophets have gone out into the world.... You are of God, little children, and have overcome them, because He who is in you is greater than he who is in the world.

—1 John 4:1, 4

❧ What does it mean to "test the spirits"? In practical terms, how does a parent do this?

❧ What encouragement does John offer to parents in this verse, when it comes to "testing the spirits"?

# God's Power Is Greater

Second, Jesus said to the Pharisees, "If I cast out demons by Beelzebub, by whom do your sons cast them out? Therefore they shall be your judges" (Matthew 12:27). A number of Jews attempted to cast out demons using a variety of exorcism methods that had been sanctioned by the Pharisees. Jesus argued, "If it is casting out demons that is under question here, then what about those who are casting out demons under *your* authority?" He then went on, "But if I cast out demons by the Spirit of God, surely the kingdom of God has come upon you" (Matthew 12:28).

The principle is this: God has the power to cast out demons. Satan may have authority over his own demons, but he does not have *absolute* authority over them. In other words, Satan cannot rescue his demons from the greater power of God. Believers in Christ Jesus *can* cast out demons in the name of Jesus and by the power of the Holy Spirit. The ultimate authority over evil is God.

Many Christians seem confused on that point today. They seem to think that Satan's power is just as potent as God's power. That is not what the Bible teaches. God's power is absolute. He is *omnipotent—all*-powerful. God has authority over Satan. His power cannot even be compared to Satan's power. God has allowed Satan to have a limited degree of influence on this earth as a part of giving mankind free will—Satan has the power to tempt and to oppress. But all of Satan's power must be confined to the limits that God puts upon him.

What does this mean to us today with regard to our families? It means that when we rely upon God, through His Son, Jesus Christ, we are tapping into a power source that is greater than evil power. The Word of God against Satan in our families is stronger than the word of the devil, whispered in the ears of the unsuspecting and weak. For Jesus

15

to have healed a man who was demon-possessed, blind, and mute, He had to be stronger than the powers that were holding the man in his bondage.

> Then I heard a loud voice saying in heaven, "Now salvation, and strength, and the kingdom of our God, and the power of His Christ have come, for the accuser of our brethren, who accused them before our God day and night, has been cast down. And they overcame him by the blood of the Lamb and by the word of their testimony, and they did not love their lives to the death.
>
> —Revelation 12:10-11

☙ Who is "the accuser of our brethren"? What does this description tell us about him?

☙ Give practical examples of overcoming Satan through "the blood of the Lamb," your own "word of testimony," and not loving your life "to the death."

## ∽ The Greater Power of Love ∽

One of the greatest powers that God has given us for *good* is the power to love. Those who truly love are powerful forces for God and for good. What we say in love brings about *good* things. What we do out of unconditional love brings about *good* situations and relationships. God honors all that we say and do when we are motivated by love for Him and love for others, even if we make mistakes at times in *how* we show our love. Never be afraid to love others. Your expression of love will ultimately result in both harmony and a defeat of Satan.

It is out of genuine love for our families that we come to the position of saying: "I choose to love my family, and I will not allow us to be divided. We *will* come to know God and to base our lives upon His Word. We *will* become one in the Spirit." It is out of love that we are to combat the forces of evil that come our way, in effect declaring to the spirit realm, "I love my family to the point that I will lay down my very life if necessary to see Satan defeated."

Love must become the motivating force behind our desire to have a strong family. Without love, we will not pay the price of denying self, which is required if we are to live in unity and harmony with one another. Without love, we will not pay the price of time, energy, and spiritual purity required to engage in spiritual warfare on one another's behalf. Every family that I know can use more love—both love of God and love for one another. It is when we fail to love that we fail to agree, and we fail to experience victory over the enemy of our souls and our families.

Our love is always to be a reflection of God's love. It is out of God's goodness that He loves. It is out of God's presence within us that we have the capacity and the courage to love. Any time that we are in a situation that may "tear us apart," we must turn to God and say, "Let me experience more of Your love."

This is My commandment, that you love one another as I have loved you. Greater love has no one than this, than to lay down one's life for his friends.

—John 15:12-13

&. In practical terms, how might you be asked to "lay down your life" for your family this week?

&. In what ways did your parents do that for you?

By this you know the Spirit of God: Every spirit that confesses that Jesus Christ has come in the flesh is of God, and every spirit that does not confess that Jesus Christ has come in the flesh is not of God. And this is the spirit of the Antichrist, which you have heard was coming, and is now already in the world.

—1 John 4:2-3

In practical terms, how do these verses help you to "test the spirits" when it comes to deciding how to spend time and money and priorities for your family?

What pressures and "temptations" for your family are from things that don't "confess that Jesus Christ has come in the flesh"?

## Today and Tomorrow

*TODAY:* GOD'S POWER IS INFINITE, AND LOVE IS HIS GREATEST WEAPON.

*TOMORROW:* I WILL ASK HIM TO TEACH ME THIS WEEK HOW TO "LAY DOWN MY LIFE" FOR MY FAMILY.

# LESSON 3

# Stewardship of the Family

---
### ❧ In This Lesson ❧

*LEARNING:* HOW AM I TO TEACH MY CHILDREN?

*GROWING:* WHAT RELATIONSHIP SHOULD I HAVE WITH MY SPOUSE?
---

So often we think of stewardship as relating only to the giving of our time, talents, and resources to God and the church. Stewardship, however, is a much broader concept. It refers to the "caretaking" of anything that God has given to us. Certainly that is a concept that relates to our families!

## Family Is a Gift from God

Two central principles related to stewardship have a direct bearing on the family:

1. Our children and families are entrusted to us as a highly valuable gift from God, and we are commanded to care for those things that God gives us.

2. We must give an account for our stewardship of our families.

### ∽ God's Gift ∽

Our families are God's gift to us, and every child is a gift from God. How much stronger our commitment to family would be if we truly saw our families from God's perspective and *cared* for our families as our most treasured possession. Many parents today think of their children more as a burden than a gift. They see their children as "costing" them their freedom, interfering with their careers, or being a burden to them financially. Sadly, a child senses these attitudes. Those who consider their children to be a burden are likely to reject their children. Consider the impact upon a child of the three statements below:

1. "Get out of my way while I'm working" or "while I'm fixing dinner."

2. "I don't have time for you right now."

3. "You can't do this—let me do it."

Each of these statements sends a message to a child, "Stay away from me because you are a burden to me" or "You hinder me." Certainly our heavenly Father *never* treats us that way when we come to Him. He always has time for us, wants to be involved with us, and allows us to be a part of His work on this earth—even if we aren't perfect and don't do things perfectly. God never rejects us. And in like manner, we are never to reject our children or a spouse. To do so is to fail to see that person as a gift of God to your life.

∽ When have you been treated more as a burden than a "gift"? How did you feel?

If someone says, "I love God," and hates his brother, he is a liar; for he who does not love his brother whom he has seen, how can he love God whom he has not seen?

—1 John 4:20

🐦 How does this verse apply to you and your family?

🐦 Is your relationship with family members characterized more by "love" or by "hatred"?

Eve declared when she gave birth to Cain, "I have acquired a man from the LORD" (Gen. 4:1). Eve clearly perceived that her son was a gift from God—not an accident of nature, not an ill-timed conception, not a deed of man. This is the proper perspective that we are to have of our children. They are God's creation, entrusted to us as His *gift*.

### ∽ **We Are Accountable** ∽

Furthermore, God holds us accountable for all that He entrusts to us. This is not only true of the material and financial blessings that we receive, but also of the great blessing of family.

Read Matthew 25:14-29 with your *family* in mind.

∽ In what way is your family similar to the "talents" that are mentioned in this parable?

∽ In the past week, have you been "investing your talents" or wasting them? How can you improve this coming week?

Now certainly we aren't to "trade" our children or to "bury" them; furthermore, God does not take our children from us and give them to others. But note these strong teachings about our children that we can draw from this parable:

**23**

*First, God gives us our children so that we might "develop" them.* We are responsible for seeing that our children are trained up in the ways of godliness. We are also called to build up our children and to "multiply" within them the truth of God's Word. This does not happen when we say to our children:

- "Can't you ever do anything right?"

- "I don't think you'll ever amount to anything."

- "Why can't you be more like your brother or sister?"

- "You are an embarrassment to me."

- "We never wanted you in the first place."

Statements such as those do anything *but* build up a child! To a great degree, they "bury" children in a belief that they are of no value in God's eyes.

*Second, God holds us accountable for the way that we treat our children.* He will ask us when we stand before Him in heaven, "Where is your child?" God's number-one expectation of us is that we will raise our children to love and serve Him and to be faithful followers of His Word—all the way into eternity!

*Third, God enlarges our personal witness to others on the basis of how we treat our family members.* Our families are to be our number-one mission field. It is to our families that we are to show God's love and to express our faith in God. God allows our witness and ministry to be effective to others outside our family based upon how we treat our family members. The person who cannot show God's love at home is one that God cannot trust fully to show His love to the world.

Whoever receives one little child like this in My name receives Me. Whoever causes one of these little ones who believe in Me to sin, it would be better for him if a millstone were hung around his neck, and he were drowned in the depth of the sea.

—Matthew 18:5-6

ᔓ Give practical examples of what it means to "receive a child in Jesus' name."

ᔓ In what ways might a parent cause his children to sin?

Every child needs to grow up knowing:

&. "You *are* somebody! You have been gifted and blessed by God in unique and wonderful ways."

&. "You *count*; you are important to God and to me. God has a special place for you in His kingdom."

&. "You have a great capacity to bring glory to God."

&. "You are wanted by me and by God. I will do my best to care for you on this earth and to lead you to a lasting faith in Christ."

&. "God has an eternal home for you in heaven, and He is with you always to care for you, protect you, and to provide for you."

Make these the messages that you give to your children today. They are messages strongly rooted in God's love. They are messages that build a relationship with Christ. A child who grows up having these truths taught on a daily basis in the home will be assured of God's greatness and goodness. Such a child *will* bless the world.

Judge not, and you shall not be judged. Condemn not, and you shall not be condemned. Forgive, and you will be forgiven.

—Luke 6:37

❧ Give practical examples of ways that you sometimes tend to "judge" or "condemn" your family members.

❧ Give examples of people who have forgiven you in the past.

## Your Child Will Do What You Do

Your child will view himself as you view him. He will "model" your behavior. This is a vital principle for you to see in your stewardship of your family. We must not only be "speakers" of the truth to our children, but "doers" of the truth. What your child sees you do, your child will do. As you value your relationship to other family members, so your child will value his relationship to you and to others. As you value your relationship with God, so your child will come to value his relationship with God.

Jesus taught that none of us can be "greater" than those who teach us (John 13:16). Your child, therefore, is not likely to be a better parent or a better Christian than you are (unless he has a teacher or role model later in life who is highly influential). You are responsible for teaching your child how to respond to life in a godly manner. That is what has been entrusted to you. That is what God holds you accountable for doing! You are entrusted with teaching *by example* those things that are of greatest value in life: how to love God and others, how to have faith in God, how to live in daily relationship with the Holy Spirit. You are accountable for teaching your child these lessons.

> For I have given you an example, that you should do as I have done to you. Most assuredly, I say to you, a servant is not greater than his master; nor is he who is sent greater than he who sent him. If you know these things, blessed are you if you do them.

> —John 13:15-17

❧ What "example" is Jesus referring to here? (See the context of John 13 for more information.) What does this example mean in your own family life?

❧ In what ways are we not "greater" than Jesus? In practical terms, what does this mean regarding your family relationships?

### ◌◌ Teaching as You Go ◌◌

What we teach our children must be rooted in daily experience. Deuteronomy 6:6–7 says, "These words which I command you today shall be in your heart. You shall teach them diligently to your children, and shall talk of them when you sit in your house, when you walk by the way, when you lie down, and when you rise up." We are to teach our children in the home and as we go about our daily work and responsibilities, from dawn to dusk. The lessons that we teach our children are to be rooted in *daily life*. They are to be practical lessons—God's truth in *action*.

In the end, stewardship is not something that we do primarily with our words. It is something that we do first and foremost with our deeds.

> But be doers of the word, and not hearers only, deceiving yourselves. For if anyone is a hearer of the word and not a doer, he is like a man observing his natural face in a mirror; for he observes himself, goes away, and immediately forgets what kind of man he was. But he who looks into the perfect law of liberty and continues in it, and is not a forgetful hearer but a doer of the work, this one will be blessed in what he does.
>
> —James 1:22-25

◌ Give some practical examples from your own life of times when you have been a "hearer" but not a "doer." Which characterizes your family life lately?

🕿 What is "the perfect law of liberty"? How does this "law" influence your relationships with family members?

## The "Role Model" that We Give Our Children

As parents, we are entrusted with the responsibility for modeling two sets of behaviors to our children:

🕿 We are to be role models of both a marital and a parental role. (Family Relationship Role Model)

🕿 We are to be role models of a "Christian in action." (Spiritual Role Model)

You are responsible for teaching your child what it means to be a husband or a wife, and also what it means to be a parent. Nobody can teach these lessons as well as you do! Long after your child is grown, a "tape" of your example will play in your child's mind, saying, "This is how I should respond to my spouse. This is how I should act as a parent."

You are also responsible for teaching your child how to be a Christian—not only what it means to believe in Christ Jesus, but what it means to have a daily walk of obedience to God's Word. God has entrusted you to teach these lessons well and in full accordance with His Word!

### ∞ Marital Roles ∞

The Bible states very clearly the basics for being a good spouse and parent.

Read Ephesians 5:22–33:

🖎 How do you feel about the concept of a wife "submitting" to her husband? Give practical examples of what Paul is talking about.

🖎 What does it mean for a man to "love his wife as Christ loved the church"? Give practical examples of what Paul is talking about.

Note these specifics: Wives are to love and respect their husbands as they love and respect Christ Jesus. They are to be helpmeets to their husbands in all aspects of life. Husbands are to love, provide for, protect, and serve their wives, just as Christ loves, provides for, protects,

**31**

and serves us—even to the laying down of His life. Husbands are to be the spiritual decision makers or "heads" of the family, even as they take their "marching orders" from God. Wives are to submit to their husbands in this, just as the church submits to God. In all ways, Christ is to be our model, and our behavior toward one another as spouses is to reflect His relationship to the church.

Through the years, I have counseled a number of young people who were raised in a home where the father was passive and the mother was domineering—in other words, homes in which the roles described above were reversed. What has been the result in the lives of the children? I've seen mental illness, including a great deal of schizophrenia, eating disorders, self-abusive behaviors and addictions, and depression. I've witnessed in these young people homosexuality and other forms of perverse sexual behavior, including promiscuity and pornography. I've seen young people who reenact a pattern of marital discord in their own families.

We cannot improve upon God's order for husband and wife relationships. We can, however, obey God's commandments in this and see healthy, fruitful behavior in our children!

≈ Does your own marriage reflect the "role models" which Paul describes? How might you improve in that area?

## ∞ Parental Role Modeling ∞

As a parent, you are to act in such a way that you "do not provoke your children to wrath, but bring them up in the training and admonition of the Lord" (Eph. 6:4). The best way *not* to provoke a child to wrath (to angry behavior rooted in bitterness) is to show and tell a child how much you love him. Don't be hesitant or stingy in telling your child, "I love you." Every child needs to hear that message often, no matter how old he may be. Don't withhold your hugs and tender kisses. A child needs to know that you value a closeness of relationship.

I have often asked teens who have become involved in immorality, "Tell me about your father." Not one has ever said to me, "My dad really loved me." Fathers especially need to learn how to express love to their children—both in verbal and nonverbal ways. Your child needs to experience the warmth of your feelings! A child who grows up feeling the unconditional love of a parent will express that love to others— including his own child someday.

∞ Did you know the warmth of a parent's affection as a child?

∞ How often do you tell your children that you love them? How about your spouse?

## ∞ Modeling the Christian Life ∞

Paul wrote that we are to bring up our children in the "training and admonition" of the Lord (Ephesians 6:4). In other words, we are to teach them Christian disciplines. To train is to teach by *doing*. Training does not involve theory alone—it requires *practice*. To "admonish" your child in the Lord is to require your child to engage in Christian practice. Your child may not fully understand various Christian disciplines, such as prayer, attending church, reading the Bible, or giving, but he does have the capability to *practice* these disciplines. Over time, he will acquire more and more meaning related to them.

Paul wrote to Timothy, "But you must continue in the things which you have learned and been assured of, knowing from whom you have learned them, and that from childhood you have known the Holy Scriptures, which are able to make you wise for salvation through faith which is in Christ Jesus" (2 Timothy 3:14–15). As parents, we are to teach *by our examples* what we value about:

- Money
- Prayer
- The church
- Personal liberty
- Non-Christians

- The Bible
- Friends
- Those in authority
- A walk of faith
- Family Members

Children, of course, are quick to spot hypocrisy. We must do what we say we believe. For example, your child will be quick to observe any difference that may exist between what you say about money and how you handle money, including the tithe and gifts that you give to the church. A child will note immediately if you value church attendance or involvement with other believers. We must be consistent in our behavior.

If you want your child to grow up attending church, then attend church faithfully as a family. If you want your child to have a strong prayer life, then pray often with your child. Let him learn how to pray by hearing you pray. If you want your child to learn how to relate in a loving way to those in the church, let him accompany you as you help with church activities and as you participate in outreach ministries. If you want your child to grow up knowing the Bible and following its teachings, then you must read the Bible with your child and let him see that you are studying the Bible and attempting to apply its truth to your life on a daily basis. What your child sees you do and what your child is *included in doing with you* will be what your child later does as an adult.

Above all, model forgiveness to your child. Be quick to say, "I'm sorry" or to admit, "I was wrong" and to ask your child, "Please forgive me." The child who grows up with a strong role model in this area will be quick to make amends with others and quick to seek God's forgiveness for his own sin.

> The things which you learned and received and heard and saw in me, these do, and the God of peace will be with you.
>
> —Philippians 4:9

❧ Give practical examples of ways that a child will do the following: learn; receive; hear; see. What things are *YOUR* children learning from you?

Behold, children are a heritage from the LORD, The fruit of the womb is a reward.

—Psalm 127:3

☙ In practical terms, what does it mean that *YOUR* children "are a heritage from the Lord"?

☙ In the past week, which characterized your views on your family more often: "heritage from the Lord," "a true reward," "a millstone around my neck," other?

And whenever you stand praying, if you have anything against anyone, forgive him, that your Father in heaven may also forgive you your trespasses. But if you do not forgive, neither will your Father in heaven forgive your trespasses.

—Mark 11:25-26

Put these verses into your own words. How do these verses apply to your family?

Is there someone in your family that you need to forgive today? What will you do about it tomorrow?

## Today and Tomorrow

*TODAY:* MY CHILDREN WILL LEARN MORE FROM WHAT I *DO* THAN FROM WHAT I *SAY.*

*TOMORROW:* I WILL ASK THE LORD TO SHOW ME AREAS WHERE I NEED TO MAKE WORDS AND ACTIONS CONSISTENT.

**37**

# LESSON 4

# Loving Your Family Unconditionally

──────── ❧ **In This Lesson** ☙ ────────

*LEARNING:* WHAT IS UNCONDITIONAL LOVE?

*GROWING:* HOW CAN A PERSON EVER HOPE TO LOVE UNCONDITIONALLY?

Few things do as much for a person as unconditional love! Unconditional love is one of the greatest gifts that you can ever give to another person. Love is the message underlying the gospel: "For God so *loved* the world that He *gave* His only begotten Son" (John 3:16). When you truly love another person, you will be motivated to share the gospel of Jesus Christ with him, and to *live* the gospel in your relationship with him. Love compels us to keep God's commandments so that our relationships with God and other people might become deeper and more fulfilling. Love is the proper motivation for giving and forgiving.

Unconditional love is a "regardless" love: we choose to love regardless of another person's dress, hairstyle, choice of music—regardless of *any* behavior that the person might display. We love regardless of the other person's successes or failures in life. We love regardless of what another person says or does to us. Genuine unconditional love is love with no "ifs" or other qualifiers. It is love rooted solely in the fact that we choose to love.

Unconditional love is impossible without first having a sense that you are loved. Whether your parents did or did not give you that kind of love, it is vitally important that you receive God's unconditional love. As John tells us, "We love Him because He first loved us" (1 John 4:19).

🙠 When have you experienced unconditional love?

And we have known and believed the love that God has for us. God is love, and he who abides in love abides in God, and God in him.

—1 John 4:16

🙠 What does it mean to "abide in God"? How does a person do that?

🙠 Why is it essential that we first learn to love God before we can unconditionally love people?

## How Do We Show Unconditional Love?

In a previous lesson, we discussed the great importance of love for your family. In this lesson, we will deal with the practicalities of loving your family unconditionally. Our key question is this: "How might we show unconditional love to our family members?"

*First, unconditional love causes us to want to know others as unique creations of God.* One of the foremost ways that you can show love to your spouse or your child is to make a diligent effort to *understand* your spouse or child. Peter admonishes husbands to take this attitude toward their wives: "Dwell with them with understanding" (1 Peter 3:7).

Every person is a beloved and one-of-a-kind creation of God. Each person has been given specific gifts, talents, desires, abilities, and callings. When we recognize the uniqueness of those in our family, we should stand in awe of God's creativity. He has made each person special in wonderful ways. Unconditional love says, "I am glad that God made you the way you are and has placed you into my life." Our thanksgiving is to God; our appreciation is to Him.

Certainly we are to discern between good and evil and between right and wrong behaviors. Behaviors are learned, and they can be changed. We must not accept willful behavior as endorsed by God. As much as we discern willful behavior, however, we are also to discern the wonderful inherent and God-given traits of a person—those characteristics that truly make the person who he is. These are things that cannot be changed (within limits)—they can only be *developed* and *used.*

In showing God's unconditional love to others, we are wise to help them discover and develop their own talents, using them for God's glory. That is the role that parents are privileged to play in the lives of their children: see your child as God sees your child and help your child fulfill his God-ordained destiny.

> Then God saw everything that He had made, and indeed it was very good.

> —Genesis 1:31

👁 Do you believe that God created every person on earth—including your family members? How can this knowledge help you to love your family more unconditionally?

👁 God declared His creation "very good" before Adam brought sin and death into the world. How does a parent draw lines between the "very good" and the "not so good" aspects of children's behavior? How can you draw this line while still loving unconditionally?

*Second, we are called to listen to others intently.* We show uncondi-tional love to our spouse and children when we listen to them fully—to listen with interest and not out of obligation, to listen because we value them as individuals. Certainly God loves us this way. He is always available to us when we pray; no subject is off-limits with Him. We only have to read the Psalms to see that the psalmist felt very free in pouring out all of his emotions and opinions to God—nothing was held back! In fact, David referred to God as "You who hear prayer" (Psalm 65:2).

We show love to our family members when we choose to hear them as God hears them—any time of day or night, regardless of circumstances, never viewing their conversation as an interruption or an annoyance. A child or spouse will feel wanted and valued—respected—when he has a full opportunity for expression without condemnation.

A study done at the University of Michigan showed that working moth-ers spend only about eleven minutes a day of "quality time" with their children, and working fathers only about eight minutes a day. Of this time, only about half of it is spent listening to a child. The time spent on weekend days was only thirty minutes for mothers and fourteen min-utes for fathers. That simply isn't enough listening time if you want to express love to your child! In listening intently to your family mem-bers:

      look them in the eye, face-to-face

      don't interrupt or change the subject

      ask questions and do your best to answer their questions

      seek out their opinions regarding family-related decisions

Remember always that it is not how *we* perceive ourselves as listeners that counts; it is how our family members perceive *us* as listeners. Spend time with your spouse and children; listen to what they have to say with the intention of understanding them better.

> ...For the LORD has heard the voice of my weeping. The LORD has heard my supplication; the LORD will receive my prayer.
>
> —Psalms 6:8-9

Give examples of times when you find it hard to listen to family members. How does this compare with God's attitude in listening to us?

Why is listening intently vitally important to understanding a person? Why do we often find it hard to truly listen intently?

*Third, we must not let the "performance" or behavior of a spouse or child influence our love.* Unconditional love is given without regard to whether the goal was reached, the touchdown was scored, the "A" was earned, or the dinner was perfectly cooked. Conditional love, in comparison, is based upon the philosophy of "I will love you if you do what I expect you to do."

God's blessings and chastisements are based upon our performance in keeping His commandments, but His love and forgiveness are never based upon performance! His love is motivated solely by His *desire* to love. The same must be true for us. We can reward or chastise our children based upon their performance in keeping certain family rules, but we must never withhold our love, *regardless* of behavior.

Consider two of the best things that you can do for your child:

1. Challenge your child to do his personal best rather than strive to achieve group-related goals.

2. Seek out activities that are at the level of your child's ability so that your child has a good opportunity to succeed at what he attempts.

God never gave His people laws or commandments that were beyond their ability to keep. He always *expected* them to keep His laws—they were well within human ability to perform. Furthermore, God always calls us to be our moral best. He challenges us to excel in righteousness and faithfulness, not necessarily to be a success in the eyes of others.

How have you felt in the past when someone stopped "loving" you because of a failure or lack of success?

> Yes, I have loved you with an everlasting love; Therefore with lovingkindness I have drawn you.
>
> —Jeremiah 31:3

How does God's "lovingkindness" draw others to Him? How might your lovingkindness draw your family toward God and you?

The Bible teaches that *nothing* can separate us from God's love. In Romans 8:35 we read, "Who shall separate us from the love of Christ? Shall tribulation, or distress, or persecution, or famine, or nakedness, or peril, or sword?" The answer that Paul gives is a resounding no! We must have this same stance regarding our family: that no outside situation, crisis, or need will be allowed to quench the love that we have for our family. No matter what behavior problem may exist in the life of a family member, you must not let that problem separate you or divide you in your love. In fact, unconditional love is very likely one of the strongest factors that will help you and your family members overcome behavioral problems by seeking out godly solutions.

> As the Father loved Me, I also have loved you; abide in My love.
>
> —John 15:9

ஃ What does it mean to "abide" in Christ's love? How is this done?

ஃ Give practical examples of how "abiding in the love of God" will affect your love for your family.

## Unconditional Love Leads Us to Forgive

It is out of unconditional love that we are able to forgive others, regardless of the offense or sin against us. Even when we are faced with hatred, anger, or rejection, we are capable of forgiving if we truly have unconditional love in our hearts. Jesus taught very clearly, "Forgive, and you will be forgiven" (Luke 6:37). Furthermore, He taught that it is *only* as we forgive others that we are capable of receiving God's full forgiveness for our own sins (Mark 11:25–26).

Unconditional love and a quickness to forgive go hand in hand. If we withhold forgiveness, we are saying to others, "My love for you is related to what you do and don't do." That is conditional love, not unconditional love. Withholding forgiveness brings about a feeling of shame; shame and love are never compatible.

> But if you love those who love you, what credit is that to you?
> For even sinners love those who love them.
>
> —Luke 6:32

❧ When have you tried in the past to love someone who hated you? What was the result?

And whenever you stand praying, if you have anything against anyone, forgive him, that your Father in heaven may also forgive you your trespasses. But if you do not forgive, neither will your Father in heaven forgive your trespasses.

—Mark 11:25-26

☙ How does forgiveness influence our ability to love others unconditionally? Give practical examples.

## Unconditional Love is a Choice of the Will

Ultimately, unconditional love is a choice of your will. It is not a feeling as much as it is an act of *choosing* to respond to another person as God responds to that person. It is choosing to see another person through God's eyes and then relating to that person as God wants you to relate to him. Read again these verses from the famous "love chapter" of 1 Corinthians 13:1-8, and, as you read, relate it to your own family relationships:

Though I speak with the tongues of men and of angels, but have not love, I have become sounding brass or a clanging cymbal. And though I have the gift of prophecy, and understand all mysteries and all knowledge, and though I have all faith, so that I could remove mountains, but have not love, I am nothing. And though I bestow all my goods to feed the poor, and though I give my body to be burned, but have not love, it profits me nothing. Love suffers long and is kind; love does not envy; love does not parade itself, is not puffed up; does not behave rudely, does not seek its own, is not provoked, thinks no evil; does not rejoice in iniquity, but rejoices in the truth; bears all things, believes all things, hopes all things, endures all things. Love never fails.

≈ Put the following aspects of love into your own words, and give real-life examples of each.

Suffers long

Is kind

Does not envy

Does not parade itself

Does not behave rudely

Does not seek its own

Thinks no evil

Rejoices in the truth

Love has been perfected among us in this: that we may have boldness in the day of judgment; because as He is, so are we in this world. There is no fear in love; but perfect love casts out fear, because fear involves torment. But he who fears has not been made perfect in love.

—1 John 4:17-18

‸ What does John mean when he says, "because as He is, so are we in this world"? What characterizes God? How do we reflect that in this world?

‸ Give examples of "fear in love". How can a parent "cast out" such fear from a child?

My little children, let us not love in word or in tongue, but in deed and in truth.

—1 John 3:18)

☙ Give examples of how people might "love in word" without loving "in deed". Does this characterize the love that *you* have for your family?

☙ Give examples of how a person loves "in deed and in truth". What is the difference between "deed" and "truth"? How can you develop this love for your family this week?

## ☙ Today and Tomorrow ❧

*TODAY:* UNCONDITIONAL LOVE MEANS THAT I LISTEN TO AND ACCEPT OTHERS, REGARDLESS OF CIRCUMSTANCES.

*TOMORROW:* I WILL ASK THE LORD TO TEACH ME TO LOVE OTHERS THIS WEEK IN THE WAY THAT HE LOVES ME.

# Lesson 5

# Keeping Safe from Spiritual Bondage

## *Part 1*

━━━━━━━━━ ⌘ **In This Lesson** ⌘ ━━━━━━━━━

*Learning:* Why can't I break out of my sinful habits?

*Growing:* Who is responsible for the attitudes of my children?

Perhaps the foremost challenge that we face as parents today is to *keep* our families out of spiritual bondage. At the root of virtually every form of family dysfunction and disharmony, one finds a form of spiritual bondage. Name any problem that plagues the family today and you will find that the problem actually began in the spiritual realm. It had its seed of beginning in the heart of one person's rebellion against God. Many forms and sources of bondage plague the family today. The vast majority of them do not involve demonic *possession,* but they all involve some form of demonic *oppression* and deceit. In this lesson we will deal with three elements that can lead to spiritual "entrapment" by the enemy:

1. The lies of Satan.

2. Willful sin.

3. Not guarding our lives against evil.

# The Lies of Satan Entrap Us

The lies of Satan are a trap. A multitude of lies serve as tiny threads that encircle the spirit—round and round and round—until the person is trapped, oppressed, and "bound." Most of the lies that Satan speaks to us are not giant "ropes." If they were, we would recognize them immediately and reject them. Rather, his lies often seem to be innocent little "white lies," small errors against God's Word. These lies are like hundreds of tiny threads that bind us spiritually. If you wrap enough sewing thread around a person, you can entrap him just as securely as if you wrapped a few heavy ropes around him.

Some families are in bondage because the father is an alcoholic, enslaved to a chemical that can destroy himself and his entire family. Somewhere along the line, this father believed the lie, "One little drink won't hurt you." And then another lie: "A few drinks never hurt anybody, and they won't hurt you." And then another lie: "You are in control of your drinking, and as long as you are in control, you are all right." And then another lie and another until the man was in bondage, no longer in control of his drinking or his resulting negative behavior. He eventually entered a state of oppression that affected his family and put his wife and children into a form of bondage as well.

Some families are in bondage to bitterness. Consider a mother, for example, who has a deep-seated bitterness toward her husband or to another person. She once bought a lie of Satan: "You have justification to be bitter and to harbor this anger and hatred in your heart." That lie led to another: "How you feel is your business alone. Your feelings don't affect your husband or your children." And the lies continued as the bitterness built. The result, however, is now a family in which both husband and children "tiptoe" around Mom because nobody is quite sure what will set her off or how her bitterness will be spewed out against them. Such a family is in bondage—not free in spirit, not honest in communication, not genuinely loving in an unconditional, generous way.

Some families are in bondage to pornography, an illicit sexual affair, or a spirit of greed. Jealousy, a sensual spirit, and a lust for material goods all can result in great personal and family bondage. Numerous forms of maladjustment and dysfunction result in bondage. All, however, began with a lie or a deceitful temptation of Satan.

When we are tempted by Satan and yield to that temptation, it is as if we open the door to our lives and our families and invite Satan to enter. If Satan can get one member of the family, and especially so the father, he has entry to the entire family. A man who willingly and repeatedly yields to Satan's temptation has no authority to keep Satan out of the lives of the rest of his family members.

&. When have you experienced bondage in your family? Can you identify the initial lie of Satan that caused that bondage?

[The devil] was a murderer from the beginning, and does not stand in the truth, because there is no truth in him. When he speaks a lie, he speaks from his own resources, for he is a liar and the father of it.

—John 8:44

෨ What "little lies" have you chosen to believe in your life? How have those lies led to more significant problems?

## Sin Puts Us in Bondage

A prevailing truth in God's Word is this: sin creates spiritual bondage. Many other factors may contribute to bondage, but sin against God is the central factor that creates the spiritual bondage which gives rise to both personal and family problems. Can a person sin repeatedly and not experience bondage? No. A pattern of sin in a person's life will always result in bondage, which is also described in the Bible as enslavement or "dominion."

Romans 6:13–16 tells us:

> And do not present your members as instruments of unrighteousness to sin, but present yourselves to God as being alive from the dead, and your members as instruments of righteousness to God. For sin shall not have dominion over you, for you are not under law but under grace. What then? Shall we sin because we are not under law but under grace? Certainly not! Do you not know that to whom you present yourselves slaves to obey, you are that one's slaves whom you obey, whether of sin leading to death, or of obedience leading to righteousness?

A number of people have confessed to me that they *knew* they were sinning from the outset, but they tried to convince themselves, "I'll stop this after a while. One of these days, I'll turn around and break loose of this." They felt that they had power over sin. The truth of God's Word is that the impulses which a person obeys and the desires that a person acts upon have power over that person. In the case of alcohol, the person takes a drink, and the desire increases. Eventually the drink takes over the person. Another person feels anger and hate. The anger and hatred build and eventually dictate what the person does, perceives, feels, and thinks.

Bondage begins when we sin against God. It becomes increasingly entrenched the longer we continue in the sin.

> For the wages of sin is death, but the gift of God is eternal life in Christ Jesus our Lord.

> —Romans 6:23

❧ Why does Paul speak of the "wages of sin," rather than the "result of sin?" What does this imply?

❧ Contrast the "wages of sin" with the "gift of God." What does this imply about breaking out of sin's bondage?

## ◈ The Power of a Single Sin ◈

Massive family problems can grow from one sinful act, born of one family member's will. One person decides to do things his way, contrary to God's way. One person wants something that is born of a rebellious or proud heart—in opposition to the Word of God and God's plan for the family. I have counseled families in which the problem that threatened a marriage began with just one hurtful and unloving statement rooted in anger and bitterness. One act of infidelity. One "experimentation" with a chemical. One lie. That one willful, sinful act prompted other family members to *react* in sinful and willful ways. The problem compounded until it was so complex that it was virtually unsolvable by the human mind. Nevertheless, the problem began simply: a single act of sin.

⮢ Can you identify a problem in your family that began with a single act of rebellion against God's Word? What can you do to solve that problem?

The Bible is very clear on the fact that *all* sin has negative consequences. Ultimately, the consequence for an unredeemed sin nature is eternal death. On this earth, however, we also experience something of a "death" inside us when we sin. Sin causes a part of our soul to die—we might call it a loss of innocence, a callousness of conscience, a hardening of the heart. We experience an inner torment, which we sometimes are even hard-pressed to identify.

Never wink at sin in your life or the lives of your family members. Never say, "Oh, it was just a little lie, it was just a little angry outburst." The best time to deal with sin is at its inception. Call sin what it is—a deadly disease in both the individual's life and the life of your family. Teach your children to recognize sin and call it what it is. Be quick to respond to sin by calling a person to repentance and to a change of behavior. Be quick to ask for God's forgiveness when you sin and to pray with your children when they have sinned. The good news for each of us is that God is quick to forgive our sin when we come to Him with a humble and honest heart, admitting our sin and seeking His forgiveness.

One of the most important psalms that you should teach your children is Psalm 51, a portion of which is provided below:

Have mercy upon me, O God,
According to Your lovingkindness;
According to the multitude of Your tender mercies,
Blot out my transgressions.
Wash me thoroughly from my iniquity,
And cleanse me from my sin.

For I acknowledge my transgressions,
And my sin is always before me.
Against You, You only, have I sinned,
And done this evil in Your sight—
That You may be found just when You speak,
And blameless when You judge.

Purge me with hyssop, and I shall be clean;
Wash me, and I shall be whiter than snow.
Make me hear joy and gladness,
That the bones You have broken may rejoice.
Hide Your face from my sins,
And blot out all my iniquities.

Create in me a clean heart, O God,
And renew a steadfast spirit within me.

—Psalm 51:1–4, 7–10

≈ Note that David says to God, "Against You, You only, have I sinned." What does this tell you about giving in to temptation?

☙ How does a person gain "a clean heart" and a "steadfast spirit" after sinning?

# Giving Ready Access to Satan

At times Satan seems to enter our families through an unlocked door. On these occasions, he doesn't need to launch any major assault or even to engage in persistent temptation. It is as if we provide ready access for uninvited entry. How might this happen?

☙ By not training our children in the commandments of God.

☙ By not setting limits and boundaries.

☙ By not taking charge of our schedules and establishing our priorities so that God, His Word, and the church are of paramount importance to us as a family.

☙ By not choosing and then intentionally pursuing God's plan for authority and responsibility within the family.

The sin in this case is one of *omission*—of failing to do what is right before God. When we fail to establish good, we are open prey to evil. When we fail to set standards for righteousness, the lack of standards results in unrighteousness. At times, the unlocked door is related to things that we allow into our homes that we should not allow.

I once had a woman say to me, "I wish I could keep my fifteen-year-old son from reading a certain pornographic magazine." I said, "Don't blame your son. You have the authority to keep that magazine out of your home." She seemed stunned. "I have the authority?" she said with a giant question mark in her voice. "Yes," I said. "You have authority over your son as long as he is in your home and you are responsible for him legally, financially, socially, and morally. Those who have responsibility have authority."

### ∞ A Parent's Example Can Be an Unlocked Door ∞

At other times, the parents unwittingly set an example that leaves an unlocked door in their children's lives. They want their children to "do what they say," unaware that their children are far more likely to "do what they do." I've had parents complain to me that their children drink too much at college, but if you opened the refrigerator in their homes, you'd find a six-pack of beer. I've had parents moan that their young-adult children aren't going to church, but they do not see the relationship between their playing golf on Sunday mornings and the fact that their children aren't attending church. I've had parents cry on my shoulder that their children run with a group of kids who watch all sorts of R-rated and X-rated movies and videos, but as I question them, I find that those same parents never took control of the television dial in their own home. In fact, those same parents watch R-rated and X-rated movies and videos themselves.

As parents, we must not allow certain things into our homes, and we must be very cautious in what we ourselves do. Our children will always test the boundaries that we set. They will always copy our behavior. Any time we neglect to set proper boundaries or engage in improper behavior ourselves, we are leaving open a door that should have been locked against the enemy. We must do our utmost to "lock the doors" spiritually if we hope to deter Satan's efforts in plundering our children.

## ∽ The Primary Responsibility Belongs to Dad ∽

The father is primarily responsible for making sure that the doors of the home are locked spiritually. In Matthew 12:29 Jesus said, "How can one enter a strong man's house and plunder his goods, unless he first binds the strong man? And then he will plunder his house." The "strong man" in a family is the father. He is the one who has the ultimate responsibility for and authority over his family members.

The word *house* in this verse can refer to the family as well as to a physical structure. We find this usage in 1 Timothy 3:2, 4 where it says, "A bishop then must be blameless ... one who rules his own house well, having his children in submission with all reverence." A man does not rule his physical house, but rather, those in it; he has authority over and responsibility for the members who reside in the house. In cases where the father is not in the home, the mother has responsibility for her children. Part of that responsibility is to be an active member of a church in which the pastor and other strong Christian men can be authority figures and role models for her sons and daughters.

The word *goods* means vessels—containers of precious value. This word can refer to family members, the most precious of all treasures to a husband and father. Satan desires to "plunder" our spouses and our children.

It is very difficult for a wife and children to defend themselves against the onslaught of Satan if the father is weak spiritually or is willingly in rebellion against God. They are "open prey" to Satan's efforts. Satan will always hit the father first because he knows that if he gets the dad, he gets the family. In like manner, the father is the key to his family's salvation. In Acts 16 we read about a jailer who fell before Paul and Silas with fear and trembling, asking, "Sirs, what must I do to be saved?" They said to him, "Believe on the Lord Jesus Christ, and you will be saved, you and your household" (Acts 16:30–31).

When a man accepts Jesus as Savior and begins to follow Him as Lord, it is much easier for that man's wife and children to come to the Lord and to follow Him on a daily basis. In fact, the closer a father follows Christ, the closer his family will follow Christ. This does not mean that the children of every saved man will automatically be saved, but the chances are much greater that saved parents will raise children who will accept Christ for themselves.

⮞ What role did your father have in setting the spiritual tone for the family? What were the results?

Exhort one another daily, while it is called "TODAY," lest any of you be hardened through the deceitfulness of sin.

—Hebrews 3:13

⮞ What does it mean to become "hardened through the deceitfulness of sin"? Give examples.

 What does it mean to "exhort one another"? When should we do this?

---

###  Today and Tomorrow 

*TODAY:* PARENTS TEACH PRIMARILY BY EXAMPLE—ESPECIALLY THE FATHER—AND I MUST LEARN TO "LOCK" SATAN OUT OF THE HOME BY BEING OBEDIENT TO GOD'S WORD.

*TOMORROW:* I WILL ASK THE LORD TO SHOW ME AREAS IN MY LIFE WHICH NEED TO BE "SAFELY LOCKED UP."

---

# Keeping Safe from Spiritual Bondage

## *Part 2*

---

### ❧ In This Lesson ☙

*LEARNING:* WHAT IS THE SECRET FOR AVOIDING SPIRITUAL BONDAGE?

*GROWING:* HOW CAN I BECOME STRONGER IN MY WALK WITH GOD?

---

How can a family avoid spiritual bondage? We might conclude from our previous lesson that we should:

1. Refuse to listen to the lies of the devil (and refuse to yield to his temptations).

2. Do no sin.

3. Give no entrance to sinful influence.

A family that takes those three steps will be spared a great deal of trauma and trouble. James 4:7 gives us two further keys: "Submit to God. Resist the devil and he will flee from you."

# Submit to God

Submission to God occurs when we face up to our own sinful nature and say to God, "I am a sinner in need of Your forgiveness. Please forgive me and fill me with Your Holy Spirit so that I can change my life and live in a way that is pleasing to You." Submission is a total yielding of ourselves to God. God wants our submission to Him to be total— nothing held back. We are to give Him our talents, our timetables, our desires, our possessions, our lives, our work, our *all*.

Once we are in right relationship with God, we face a daily submission of our will. No person is capable of completely submitting all to Christ and then never having to submit again. Submission is ongoing. It requires a continual yielding of our will to His will. We must come to God every day and say, "Guide me, Holy Spirit. Lead me in the ways in which I should go. Cause me to say what I am to say, to make the decisions that are right before God, and to do the things I am to do."

> I beseech you therefore, brethren, by the mercies of God, that you present your bodies a living sacrifice, holy, acceptable to God, which is your reasonable service. And do not be conformed to this world, but be transformed by the renewing of your mind, that you may prove what is that good and acceptable and perfect will of God.
>
> —Romans 12:1-2

In practical terms, what does it mean to "present your bodies a living sacrifice" to God?

✎ How does a person renew his mind?

## ∞ Submission to God's Commandments ∞

We can be certain about this: the Holy Spirit will always lead us to live in full accordance with God's commandments. Nothing that the Holy Spirit ever directs you to say or do will be contrary to the Bible.

God has a path for you to walk. His commandments are His "limitations"—like hedges along that path. The commandments give us a clear direction about how we are to live as individuals and as families. You are wise to remind yourselves frequently *as a family* of God's commandments, and to use them as the basis for limitations on your children. As you establish rules for your child, here are some principles to follow:

*Make your instructions and rules clear.* Be precise. Speak in a language that your child understands. God has made His commandments very clear and direct in the Bible. They are readily understood. Make sure that your family rules and instructions are equally clear.

*Whenever possible, explain to your children why you are giving certain limitations.* Have a reason for your family rules. God certainly has an ultimate reason behind the commandments that He has given us. They clearly are for our good. The rules that you establish for your family should also be for good, not out of habit or from self-centered desire.

*Establish consequences for disobeying family rules.* God has told us very clearly that we will suffer consequences when we break His commandments. Match your disciplinary measures to the disobedience.

*Establish rewards for obeying family rules.* God has said in His Word that we are subject to chastisement when we disobey Him, but He has also said that He is a "rewarder" to those who are faithful in obeying Him. Your children, too, need to be rewarded and praised for their good behavior. Rewards are far more motivating than threats of punishment.

> But without faith it is impossible to please Him, for he who comes to God must believe that He is, and that He is a rewarder of those who diligently seek Him.
>
> —Hebrews 11:6

🕹 Why is it impossible to please God without faith? How does this compare with a child's desire to please his parents?

🕹 Why is it important for our faith to remember that God "is a rewarder of those who diligently seek Him"? Why is it important for children to know the same about their parents?

# Resist the Devil

Resisting the devil is sometimes as simple as just saying no to his temptations. At other times, the assault of the devil is stronger, and we must put up an even greater defense against evil. How do we do that?

**We must pray and ask God for help.** None of us are a match for the devil in our own strength. But the devil is never a match for *us and God*. Make daily prayer a habit in your family. Gather together in the morning as a family to "give your day to God." Ask for God's help, provision, and protection for the things that you are facing during the course of the day. Gather again as a family at night to thank God for being with you and ask Him to watch over you as you sleep. Let your children hear you pray, and especially let them hear (or overhear) you pray for them very personally, by name. Build into your children an understanding that you *believe* in God and that you *trust* God to help you every day of your life.

**We must learn how to use the Word of God against the devil.** Read the way in which Jesus confronted and resisted Satan when he came to Jesus in the wilderness:

> Now when the tempter came to Him, he said, "If You are the Son of God, command that these stones become bread." But He answered and said, "It is written, 'Man shall not live by bread alone, but by every word that proceeds from the mouth of God.'"

> Then the devil took Him up into the holy city, set Him on the pinnacle of the temple, and said to Him, "If You are the Son of God, throw Yourself down. For it is written: 'He shall give His angels charge over you,' and, 'In their hands they shall bear you up, lest you dash your foot against a stone.'"

Jesus said to him, "It is written again, 'You shall not tempt the LORD your God.'"

Again, the devil took Him up on an exceedingly high mountain, and showed Him all the kingdoms of the world and their glory. And he said to Him, "All these things I will give You if You will fall down and worship me.'"

Then Jesus said to him, "Away with you, Satan! For it is written, 'You shall worship the LORD your God, and Him only you shall serve.'"

—Matthew 4:3–10

✎ Examine the temptations that the devil used against Jesus, and Jesus' responses to them. What can you learn from this?

✎ What did Jesus do to resist the devil? How can you imitate His techniques?

Three times Satan came to Jesus to tempt Him, and three times Jesus resisted the devil's temptation by using the Word of God. We are wise to do the same! Of course, if we are going to use the Scriptures in resisting the devil, we must *know* the Scriptures. Make reading God's Word a daily habit in your family.

You might choose to read the Bible together as a family, or you might choose to establish a "quiet time" in which each family member reads the Word for himself. It is very helpful to some families for each person to be reading the same chapters of the Bible during "individual" daily devotions; mealtime conversations can then be focused in part on the insights into God's Word that each person gleaned.

John tells us that the temptations of Satan are focused on three areas: "the lust of the flesh, the lust of the eyes, and the pride of life" (1 John 2:16). You can count on the devil to come to you and your family and tempt you repeatedly to fulfill the lusts of your physical flesh, tempt you to fulfill your desire for more and more things, and tempt you to seek more and more status. Warn your children in advance that these temptations *will* come, and give your children the scriptural tools to counteract them. Help your child to memorize verses that speak of God's purity, God's provision, and the humility of heart that God desires for us.

> And do not present your members as instruments of unrighteousness to sin, but present yourselves to God as being alive from the dead, and your members as instruments of righteousness to God.
>
> —Romans 6:13

&#x221A; In practical terms, how does a person "present your members as instruments" to sin? As instruments of righteousness?

∾ What difference does it make in our thinking if we remember that we are "alive from the dead"? What difference does it make in our behavior?

> Let love be without hypocrisy. Abhor what is evil. Cling to what is good.
>
> —Romans 12:9

∾ In what way is love hypocritical if a person loves what is evil? Give practical examples.

∾ Why does Paul tell us to "cling to what is good"? Why didn't he just say, "love what is good"?

Be sober, be vigilant; because your adversary the devil walks about like a roaring lion, seeking whom he may devour. Resist him, steadfast in the faith, knowing that the same sufferings are experienced by your brotherhood in the world.

—1 Peter 5:8-9

In practical terms, what does it mean to be "sober" and "vigilant" against the devil?

How does knowing that other Christians suffer the same temptations help us to resist the devil?

And take the helmet of salvation, and the sword of the Spirit, which is the word of God; praying always with all prayer and supplication in the Spirit, being watchful to this end with all perseverance and supplication for all the saints.

—Ephesians 6:17-18

☙ How are helmets and swords used? What does each do? What can we learn from this about resisting the devil?

☙ How can "supplication for all the saints" help us to resist the devil?

─────── ☙ **Today and Tomorrow** ☙ ───────

*TODAY:* IF I AM TO PROTECT MY FAMILY, I MUST FIRST SUBMIT TO GOD AND RESIST THE DEVIL.

*TOMORROW:* I WILL CONSCIOUSLY OBEY GOD'S WORD THIS WEEK, AND WILL STAND FIRM AGAINST TEMPTATION.

# Laying a Firm Foundation

---

### ✎ In This Lesson ✐

*LEARNING:* What exactly should I be teaching my children?

*GROWING:* How am I to model those things in my own life?

---

We all know the old adage, "The best defense is a good offense." Proverbs 22:6 provides the good offense for protecting your family: "Train up a child in the way he should go, and when he is old he will not depart from it." Training involves two essentials:

1. A focus on teaching the "right" things to do.

2. Practice in doing the right things.

## Teaching the Right Things

In the last lesson we focused on several right things to do in your family: submit your life to God and read and study the Word of God so that you might submit to God's commandments and use the Scriptures in resisting the devil.

The greatest thing that you can ever do for your child is to share the gospel with him. Make God's plan of salvation very clear to your child—

that God sent His Son to die a sacrificial death on the cross so that your child might be freed of the penalty of death. When your child believes on Jesus Christ as Savior and receives God's forgiveness, he is spiritually reborn into the kingdom of God. At that point, the Holy Spirit indwells your child to help him live a life that is pleasing to God and that brings great blessings, now and into eternity.

A part of every parent's challenge is to prepare a child for full accountability to God. The parent's role is to guide a child to a deep inner sense of personal responsibility for his behavior, and an accountability to God for his attitudes and actions. Children are concrete thinkers, so this sense of responsibility and accountability must first be seen in the home. A child must know from infancy that he is accountable to his parents, who are responsible for him under God's authority. Increasingly, a child is to be held responsible for his own behavior and for being accountable directly to God. By the time a child reaches adulthood, he should feel completely responsible for his own life and fully accountable to God, who is the supreme authority over his life. This process is one of spiritual maturing, with the parent as chief overseer and teacher.

In teaching your child accountability to God, you also are teaching the "chain of authority" under which we all live. Every person is subject to someone, and we are all subject to God. Submission is a repeated theme in the New Testament epistles. A child who does not learn to submit to parental authority will be rebellious against all authority, and will ultimately be rebellious against God's authority. Don't let that happen! Insist that your child obey you.

Let every soul be subject to the governing authorities. For there is no authority except from God, and the authorities that exist are appointed by God. Therefore whoever resists the authority resists the ordinance of God, and those who resist will bring judgment on themselves.

—Romans 13:1-2

∽ How do these verses apply to our relations with: police? politicians? bosses?

∽ What sort of role model have your children seen in *your* relations with earthly authority figures?

### ∝ The Right Things ∝

We have considered how important it is to teach a child how to accept Christ Jesus as Savior, how to mature into accountability for his life, and how to respect authority. There are still a number of other things that are vitally important to teach your child in order to protect him from evil. Among those "right" principles are these eight:

77

1. *The sovereignty of God.* The central concept of the Bible is that there is only *one God*, sovereign and almighty. He is our creator, our provider, our sustainer, our deliverer. He is King of kings and Lord of lords.

2. *Reliability of Scripture.* As you teach your child the Bible, do so with the perspective that the Bible is true and trustworthy. Don't teach the Bible as a storybook, but as truth on which your child can base his eternal future and all of life's decisions.

> All Scripture is given by inspiration of God, and is profitable for doctrine, for reproof, for correction, for instruction in righteousness, that the man of God may be complete, thoroughly equipped for every good work.
>
> —2 Timothy 3:16-17

How do "doctrine," "reproof," and "instruction in righteousness" differ?

In what way does the Bible equip a child for "every good work"? How does this apply, for instance, to a person's career?

3. *How to forgive others*. Teach your child the importance of forgiveness, and how to ask forgiveness of others and make amends in righting wrongs.

4. *How to trust God in every circumstance*. A recent research study found that, when teens are under stress, they turn to *music* as their first resort for comfort. Mom was number 31 on the list and Dad was number 48. Counselors, teachers, and pastors were all tied at 54, which was at the bottom of the list! When tough times come, as they invariably do, your child needs to trust God and come to you as a parent for comfort and counsel. The way that you teach trust to your child is to *be* trustworthy. Keep your child's secrets, follow through on what you say you will do, and be present for your child in experiences that require courage or fortitude.

> For You, Lord, are good, and ready to forgive, and abundant in mercy to all those who call upon You.

> —Psalm 86:5

How well does your life reflect God's abundant mercy? God's readiness to forgive?

How can you improve these areas in the coming week?

5. *God's law of sowing and reaping.* God's Word is very clear: we reap what we sow; what we give, we receive. Teach your child to give generously. Reward your child for good behavior; chastise him for bad behavior. A part of your child's sowing needs to be giving to the church. Even a young child can give a tithe of his allowance. Put your child into a position of receiving the blessings associated with the tithe (Malachi 3:10–11).

6. *How to find identity in Christ Jesus.* Teach your child that he is to grow spiritually, just as he grows physically. Set the goal of Christ Jesus before him, teaching him that he is to become more and more like Christ. Help your child discover his talents, develop them fully, and then use them in some form of ministry to others.

> Give, and it will be given to you: good measure, pressed down, shaken together, and running over will be put into your bosom. For with the same measure that you use, it will be measured back to you.
>
> —Luke 6:38

❧ When has God given generously to you, to the point of "overflowing"?

❧ What "measure" do your children see *you* using when you give to others—whether with money, time, or otherwise?

7. *How to experience the work of the Holy Spirit.* The Holy Spirit works within the heart of man to reveal to us the truth—in other words, to prick our consciences of right and wrong. Teach your child to be sensitive to the working of the Holy Spirit and to act upon the impulses for good that the Holy Spirit prompts in him. Teach your child that the character traits of God's own Spirit are what God desires (Galations 5:22–23).

8. *The power of faith in Christ Jesus.* Teach your child that the most potent force within him is faith in Christ Jesus. Faith is to be exercised, to be used so that it will grow strong and become *great* faith. It is by faith that we are called to live as Christians (Romans 1:17).

> But the fruit of the Spirit is love, joy, peace, longsuffering, kindness, goodness, faithfulness, gentleness, self-control. Against such there is no law.
>
> —Galatians 5:22-23

 Consider each of the fruit of the Spirit individually. How visible is each fruit in your own life?

 Where is the emphasis in your family: on cultivating the fruit of the Spirit, or on getting ahead in life?

# The Nature of Training

The eight lessons described above are part of the *content* that we are to teach within our families. The *method* by which we are to teach, however, is *training*. Training is not merely telling principles to our children; it is rooted in doing, and especially in repetitive doing. You will not teach your child to give and receive, for example, by telling your child to give. Your child will learn this lesson as he actually gives something that is valuable to him—and not only once, but repeatedly.

You will not teach your child the sovereignty of God by taking him to church once. Your child will learn this lesson as he attends church week in and week out, year in and year out, and especially as he begins to take an active part in Bible study, praise, and various acts of worship and ministry. You will not teach your child the fruit of the Spirit by telling him what that fruit is, but by demonstrating love, joy, peace, long-suffering, kindness, goodness, faithfulness, gentleness, and self-control. You will train your child in these character traits by *insisting* that he display patience, manifest goodness, be faithful in doing what he says he will do, and in exercising self-control.

As your child grows and matures, lead your child to an understanding of what it means to "self-train," which is to set limits for oneself. Allow him to set standards and parameters for his life. For example, discuss with your child an appropriate curfew time; let him be a part of the decision-making process. Give him ample room to learn to trust God for himself—to pray for things that are important to him, to trust God for outcomes and consequences, to give a witness of his faith, to see what God will do in the lives of others, and to engage in a form of ministry that is appropriate.

Thus also faith by itself, if it does not have works, is dead. But someone will say, "You have faith, and I have works." Show me your faith without your works, and I will show you my faith by my works.

—James 2:17-18

∂ What does James mean when he says that faith is "dead" without works? How do we reconcile this with the fact that salvation is by grace alone, without any works on our part?

∂ How do we demonstrate our faith in God by the works that we do? Give practical examples.

## ∞ By the Grace of God ∞

There is no substitute for doing the "good" things that protect us from the devil and from evil in the world, but we also must acknowledge that there is no "sure formula" for keeping a child or an entire family from all harm or spiritual attack. We each are brought to the position of saying, "It is only by the grace of God." What we can say with assurance is that God is in control. He is sovereign—totally omnipotent, omniscient, omnipresent, loving, and just. Jesus Christ is victor over Satan.

In any negative situation, we can have the full confidence of these three truths:

1. *God knows what we are going through.* He may not have caused the negative situation in which we find ourselves, but He has allowed it to happen for a *good* purpose.

2. *God is with us in the circumstance that we are facing.* He never leaves us nor forsakes us (Hebrews 13:5). We can trust Him to deliver us from evil, to lead us into right decisions, and to help us overcome the troubles that seem to overwhelm us. He will help us deal with any pain or shame that we experience, and He *will* heal us and make us whole as we put our faith in Him.

3. *God's purposes will be brought to pass.* God's plan will be accomplished. He is both the author and the *finisher* of our faith (Hebrews 12:2). His methods may elude our understanding, but His purposes are sure.

> Looking unto Jesus, the author and finisher of our faith, who for the joy that was set before Him endured the cross, despising the shame, and has sat down at the right hand of the throne of God.
>
> —Hebrews 12:2

❧ Jesus "despised the shame" of the cross—yet He endured it for our sakes. How can this increase His ability to help us deal with unpleasant circumstances?

 What is the difference between "author" and "finisher"? What exactly is the "finish" of our faith?

> For we must all appear before the judgment seat of Christ, that each one may receive the things done in the body, according to what he has done, whether good or bad.
>
> —2 Corinthians 5:10

 How does this verse affect your view of Christ's authority over your life?

 In what ways does God have authority over the things that you have "done in the body"?

Do not be deceived, God is not mocked; for whatever a man sows, that he will also reap. For he who sows to his flesh will of the flesh reap corruption, but he who sows to the Spirit will of the Spirit reap everlasting life. And let us not grow weary while doing good, for in due season we shall reap if we do not lose heart.

—Galatians 6:7-9

☙ In what ways do we sometimes mock God when we give in to temptations?

☙ Give practical examples of "sowing to the flesh" and of "sowing to the spirit".

---

## ☙ Today and Tomorrow ☚

*TODAY:* THERE IS A DIFFERENCE BETWEEN "TEACHING" AND "TRAINING," AND I NEED TO DO BOTH FOR MY FAMILY.

*TOMORROW:* I WILL SPEND TIME IN THE SCRIPTURES THIS WEEK, INCORPORATING GOD'S TRUTH IN MY OWN LIFE.

# LESSON 8

# Pulling Down Strongholds

## ❧ In This Lesson ☙

*LEARNING:* WHAT IS A "STRONGHOLD"?

*GROWING:* HOW CAN I TEAR DOWN STRONGHOLDS WITHIN MY FAMILY?

A spiritual stronghold is any area of resistance against the Holy Spirit in a person's life. The apostle Paul addressed the issue of spiritual strongholds in 2 Corinthians 10:3-5:

> For though we walk in the flesh, we do not war according to the flesh. For the weapons of our warfare are not carnal but mighty in God for pulling down strongholds, casting down arguments and every high thing that exalts itself against the knowledge of God, bringing every thought into captivity to the obedience of Christ.

Note specifically that a stronghold is rooted in an "argument" against God—a mind-set or attitude that is contrary to the will of God—and in "every high thing that exalts itself against the knowledge of God," which is an attitude of pride that says, "I don't need God, and I don't need to live according to God's plan."

Every stronghold begins in our attitude; it begins in the mind and heart. The more a person argues against God and sets his pride in opposition to God, the stronger the "stronghold" becomes. Another way of thinking of a stronghold is to say that a negative, proud attitude toward God exerts a "strong hold" on a person. The person who is suffering from a spiritual stronghold is a person who is stubborn, hard-hearted, stiff-necked, and in all ways rebellious toward God. A spiritual stronghold in the life of a family member can wreak havoc on family peace and harmony. A rebel in the midst of a family causes untold grief.

The good news offered by the apostle Paul is this: we *can* pull down these strongholds.

## Being Alert to Strongholds

Every person has areas of weakness or temptations to sin in certain ways. As a parent, you are wise to identify that area of weakness as quickly as possible in your child's life. In some children, it may be anger. In others, dishonesty or lying. No two children in a family are likely to be born with the same inclination toward evil. You must deal with each child individually.

Very often, a child's inclination to sin is a reflection of a parent's inclination to sin. Be aware that your child may be mirroring *your* life. It is not enough to be honest about your child's tendency to sin; we must have the courage to be honest about our own tendency to sin and deal with it by asking God's forgiveness and help.

How can you identify an area of spiritual weakness in your child? By studying and observing him. Take time with your child. Listen intently. Look for patterns of behavior over time. Part of your role as a parent is to see your child in the context of weeks, months, and years; you are the foremost person responsible for spotting long-standing trends in your child's behavior—physically, mentally, emotionally, and spiritually.

☙ What are the areas of spiritual weakness (prideful attitudes and justifying arguments) in your own life?

☙ How have you seen your own weaknesses reflected in your children's lives?

## Help Create a New Pattern

Once you have identified areas of spiritual weakness, help your child to create a new pattern of thinking and acting. You can also help your spouse, and receive help from a spouse, in combating spiritual strongholds.

1 *Talk to your child or spouse about the strongholds that exist.* Do this in an objective and loving way, not in a judgmental or condemning man-

ner. Let your child know that you see a trend in his life, but that you love him and desire to help him overcome that area of weakness. Map out a strategy together for how you will attempt to deal with this stronghold.

 *Guard your child in areas of spiritual weakness.* This doesn't mean, of course, that you need to tiptoe around your child or attempt to isolate him from all normal experiences, but that you guard what you allow in your home and whom you allow your child to be with—such as a playmate or teammate. Keep your child from others who have the same area of spiritual weakness or pride in their lives. (Do the same for your spouse.)

 *Build up your child by praising and rewarding his attempts to do what is godly.* If your child has a tendency to lie, for example, you will want to reward him for telling the truth. If your child has a tendency to display outbursts of anger, praise and reward him for times when he displays kindness. Let your spouse know that you appreciate his efforts to break a stronghold pattern.

 *Break the cycle that builds a stronghold.* Strongholds become established when the mind tells the will to engage in a certain behavior. The end result is "feeling good," so the mind will be much more prone to tell the will to engage in that behavior again. And so the cycle goes. For example, if a child steals a piece of candy, he is likely to feel a certain degree of satisfaction and pleasure at having "gotten away with" his sin, plus he has the treat of the candy itself. A certain "high" will be registered in his mind, and he very likely will set his mind about the task of deciding what he might steal next. If that next theft is successful, it also will bring a "high"—in fact, probably a little "higher high." And so the cycle goes until the child is devising ways to steal bigger things. A stronghold has been established.

What breaks the stronghold? Making certain that the sin is punished and that there is no pleasure associated with it. Throughout the Bible, we have examples of God moving among His people in a very active way to break the spiritual strongholds that were developing in them. It is a humble spirit and a yielded heart that God desires. If you do not help your children acquire humility and a desire to "agree" with God, they will face those lessons in an increasingly strong manner from others and, ultimately, from God. Spare your child the pain associated with being hard-hearted or stiff-necked.

Can two walk together, unless they are agreed?

—Amos 3:3

&. How does this verse apply to your marriage, as you raise children? How does it apply to your relationships with your children?

## Sins of Attitude

Keep in mind that the attitude of your child is just as important as your child's behavior. In the great majority of cases, a negative attitude is a strong indicator of future bad behavior. Negative attitudes are often displayed in behaviors such as pouting, sulking, scowling, deeply sighing, and slamming doors. A child with a bad attitude very likely seeks to be left alone or to be allowed to throw a "silent tantrum." Such attitudes are the toehold that lead to a spiritual stronghold. As a parent, you are wise to chastise and correct your child's attitudes as much as you do your child's deeds. If you do not, you can count on those attitudes eventually becoming damaging behaviors.

Reward your child's good attitudes. Praise him for an attitude that is positive, kind, generous, loving, or good. Let your child know that you value and appreciate such attitudes. Attitudes are rooted in emotions as much as they are ideas. Your child will absorb the "feelings" of your family life as much as he will absorb anything that you say or do. Guard your own attitude closely. Your child will pick up on your attitude and mirror it back to you!

Many of us pass on the feelings and attitudes that we acquired as a child. We simply do as parents what we had done to us as children. Very often the feelings and attitudes that we have acquired are not godly and have no place in a Christian home. Break the cycle! Be aware of your own responses. Think back to the feelings that you had as a child. Ask yourself, "Are these wise feelings to give to my own children?"

Blessed are the poor in spirit, for theirs is the kingdom of heaven.

—Matthew 5:3

༈ What does it mean to be "poor in spirit"?

🕮 In what areas do you need to become "poor in spirit"? How can you teach this to your children this week?

# The Sin of Pride

The sin of pride is the root of every spiritual stronghold, and it is a sin common to all mankind. It is not easily confronted, because we often are too proud to admit that we have pride! Pride is difficult to remove, for it goes to the core of our very nature and what we hold to be true about ourselves. As long as we think that we can do it on our own in any area of our lives, we are guilty of pride.

Pride leads to:

🕮 self-justification for sin

🕮 excuses for bad behavior

🕮 demanding of one's own way

🕮 less regard for others

Jesus must become our role model for humility and meekness if we are to overcome pride. The Holy Spirit must become our constant source of help if we are to recognize and take a stand against pride in our lives.

In your family, do not allow your child to "justify" bad behavior by saying that "everybody is doing it" or "it wasn't all that bad." Accept no excuses for bad behavior. Refuse to allow a child to *demand* his own way by means of a temper tantrum, whining, or manipulation. Insist that each family member show respect and deference to other family members. Don't let a child set your family schedule, dominate a conversation, or destroy family gatherings through rudeness, anger, or inconsiderate behavior. Set a tone for humility in your home.

> Let this mind be in you which was also in Christ Jesus, who, being in the form of God, did not consider it robbery to be equal with God, but made Himself of no reputation, taking the form of a bondservant, and coming in the likeness of men. And being found in appearance as a man, He humbled Himself and became obedient to the point of death, even the death of the cross.
>
> —Philippians 2:5–8

✎ Give practical examples of times when having a family felt like "robbery" to you. How did pride play a role in that attitude?

✎ Give practical examples of times when you have "made yourself of no reputation" in order to serve your family. What was the result of that sacrifice?

Ask the Lord to reveal to you any strongholds that are taking shape in your life or in the lives of your family members. Then ask Him to help you to deal with those strongholds. Ask Him to reveal to you *how* you should respond, *when* you should respond, and to give you the *courage* to respond. Earlier is better than later when it comes to dealing with areas of spiritual weakness, pride, and strongholds of the mind and heart.

Keep in mind always that spiritual strongholds are not only the work of the devil in our lives, but they are the means by which the devil causes us to work on his behalf. If we truly are to protect our families from evil, then we must stop evil the instant that it strikes our minds and hearts. We must truly bring "every thought into captivity to the obedience of Christ" (2 Corinthians 10:5).

> Let nothing be done through selfish ambition or conceit, but in lowliness of mind let each esteem others better than himself. Let each of you look out not only for his own interests, but also for the interests of others.
>
> —Philippians 2:3-4

☙ How do these verses contrast with the world's teaching that we must "esteem" ourselves and love ourselves?

∽ Does your life reflect these verses, or do you tend to set your own interests above those of your family?

And after all this, if you do not obey Me, then I will punish you seven times more for your sins. I will break the pride of your power; I will make your heavens like iron and your earth like bronze.

—Leviticus 26:18-19

∽ Is your life characterized by pride or humility? What areas of pride are becoming "strongholds" in your own life?

∽ In what areas do you see strongholds developing in your children? How will you begin this week to break them down?

If My people who are called by My name will humble themselves, and pray and seek My face, and turn from their wicked
ways, then I will hear from heaven, and will forgive their sin
and heal their land.

—2 Chronicles 7:14

🖎 In what areas do you need healing from negative childhood
patterns?

🖎 How can you humble yourself before God and gain that healing this week?

---

### 🖎 Today and Tomorrow 🖎

*TODAY:* STRONGHOLDS ARE BUILT ONE BRICK AT A TIME, AND THEY ARE
TORN DOWN THE SAME WAY.

*TOMORROW:* I WILL EXAMINE MY LIFE THIS WEEK FOR AREAS OF PRIDE,
SEEKING TO SET THE INTERESTS OF OTHERS ABOVE MY OWN.

# LESSON 9

# Binding Satan

───────── ❧ **In This Lesson** ❧ ─────────

*LEARNING:* HOW CAN MY FAMILY BE MORE THAN SET FREE—HOW CAN WE
BE RESTORED?

*GROWING:* WHAT DOES "THE NAME OF JESUS" HAVE TO DO WITH BONDAGE
TO SIN?

───────── ❧ ─────────

The only true and lasting means of deliverance from bondage comes through the power of Jesus Christ. The reason for this is simple: all bondage has its root in sin and in the spiritual condition of man. Unless the bondage is broken in the spiritual realm, remnants will remain.

## ❧ More than Confession of Sin? ❧

Many people find themselves in so much bondage to Satan's lies that a simple confession of sin is not enough. They may receive God's forgiveness, but they still feel enslaved by a pattern of behavior that has become a strong habit in their lives, such as the habit of drinking, the habit of thinking ill of others, or the habit of overspending. Confession of sin and God's forgiveness bring restoration in the person's relationship with God, but it does not always bring release from sin's consequences in the person's daily life.

🔊 When have you experienced this sort of bondage in your own life? Are you still struggling with this bondage?

## Jesus Came to Set Us Free

Isaiah 61:1–3 contains a prophecy of Jesus' ministry on earth:

> The Spirit of the Lord God is upon Me, because the LORD has anointed Me to preach good tidings to the poor; He has sent Me to heal the brokenhearted, to proclaim liberty to the captives, and the opening of the prison to those who are bound; to proclaim the acceptable year of the LORD, and the day of vengeance of our God; to comfort all who mourn, to console those who mourn in Zion, to give them beauty for ashes, the oil of joy for mourning, the garment of praise for the spirit of heaviness; that they may be called trees of righteousness, the planting of the LORD, that He may be glorified.

Jesus declared that this prophecy was fulfilled in His life, and those who witnessed His ministry knew it to be true (Luke 4:16–21). As believers in Christ Jesus, we are called to carry on His ministry on this earth. The mandate given to Jesus is our mandate. Jesus said that, through the power of the Holy Spirit, we would do even "greater works" than His. He said, "He who believes in Me, the works that I do he will do also; and greater works than these he will do, because I go to My Father. And whatever you ask in My name, that I will do, that the Father may be glorified in the Son. If you ask anything in My name, I will do it" (John 14:12–14).

Jesus sent out His disciples to minister in His name. He sent them two by two, and He told them to go into a city and to proclaim the good news: that the presence, power, and peace of God were found in Jesus Christ. We are to do the same—beginning in our own families. We are to proclaim the good news that Jesus has come, that He is present with us now, and that He will defeat Satan at every turn. Jesus came to counteract the work of Satan, and we are to start that same work in our own families.

> He who sins is of the devil, for the devil has sinned from the beginning. For this purpose the Son of God was manifested, that He might destroy the works of the devil.
>
> —1 John 3:8

൷ What "works of the devil" do you see growing in your own family?

൷ If Jesus were to visit your family, what would He say or do to destroy those works? How can you imitate that for your family?

# A Threefold Purpose

Note specifically the threefold purpose of binding Satan in our families:

1. Release

2. Restoration

3. Restriction

## ∞ Release ∞

We are to "proclaim liberty to the captives, and the opening of the prison to those who are bound" (Isaiah 61:1). True freedom is only found in Christ Jesus. As we read in John 8:36, "If the Son makes you free, you shall be free indeed." We are to proclaim the gospel boldly and without hesitation. Satan cannot operate in the presence of the gospel. Revelation 12:11 assures us that we can overcome Satan by the "word of [our] testimony," which is a testimony about the power of Jesus Christ and the salvation that He purchased for us on the cross.

> The Spirit of the Lord GOD is upon Me, Because the LORD has anointed Me To preach good tidings to the poor; He has sent Me to heal the brokenhearted, To proclaim liberty to the captives, And the opening of the prison to those who are bound.
>
> —Isaiah 61:1

∞ How does the Spirit of the Lord help us to "open the prison to those who are bound"?

☙ How can you help your family to break out of prison?

## ∽ Restoration ∽

Jesus' ministry is a constant example of restoring those who were trapped by Satan—for example, those who were trapped by sickness, troubles, or demonic snares. Jesus came to restore the lost to the Father.

In Luke we read about Jesus casting a legion of demons from a man in Gadera. This man was completely delivered. He had once lived among the tombs and the hogs, but after Jesus delivered him, he was found "sitting at the feet of Jesus, clothed and in his right mind" (Luke 8:35). The man begged Jesus that he might go back with Him to the other side of the Sea of Galilee, but Jesus said, "Return to your own house, and tell what great things God has done for you" (v. 39). Jesus *restored* this man to his right mind, to a right relationship with God, and to his family. When we bind Satan, we can expect the same results!

I believe that there are many marriages that might be restored and many children who might return home to a right relationship with their parents if they could only return to parents who are truly "set free" from sin, operating in a right mind and with a right heart.

**102**

Jesus answered them, "Most assuredly, I say to you, whoever commits sin is a slave of sin. And a slave does not abide in the house forever, but a son abides forever. Therefore if the Son makes you free, you shall be free indeed."

—John 8:34-36

❧ What is the difference between a household slave and a son? How does this apply to family members who are enslaved by sin?

❧ How has God set us free from sin? Give practical examples of how we are to "tap into" this freedom.

## ∞ Restriction ∞

Jesus wants us to ask Him to restrict the power of Satan on the earth. God has given us a free will to choose God's way or the devil's way. We must voluntarily ask God to keep the devil from exercising influence on our lives and the lives of those for whom we are responsible. God certainly *can* exert authority and control over anything and over all things as He wills, but He has given us choice. He wants us to *choose* to ask Him to restrict the activity of the devil against us—to move in a mighty way against the power of the enemy. This is what we call "binding" Satan spiritually.

In reality, we are not the ones who do the actual binding. Jesus is the One who does the binding. He is the One who has defeated Satan and who is stronger than Satan on all accounts. Satan is stronger than any human being, but he is never stronger than a human being who is filled with the Holy Spirit. The power of the Holy Spirit *within us* is always more potent than the working of Satan *around us*. As 1 John 4:4 says, "He who is in you [the Holy Spirit] is greater than he [the devil] who is in the world."

> And Jesus came and spoke to them, saying, "All authority has been given to Me in heaven and on earth."
>
> —Matthew 28:18

✎ In practical terms, how can a parent use Jesus' authority to drive Satan away from the family?

# Our Binding Weapons

Jesus has given us three "weapons" by which we are to bind Satan: the Word, the Blood, and the name of Jesus.

## ◦◦ The Word ◦◦

Jesus told a parable in Matthew 13:18–24 about a sower who sowed seed with four different results:

> Therefore hear the parable of the sower: When anyone hears the word of the kingdom, and does not understand it, then the wicked one comes and snatches away what was sown in his heart. This is he who received seed by the wayside.

Jesus is saying that the first bad thing that can happen to seed is that it fails to germinate and take root—it falls onto the soil of those who are ignorant of spiritual things. In 2 Corinthians 4:3–4, Paul wrote, "If our gospel is veiled, it is veiled to those who are perishing, whose minds the god of this age has blinded, who do not believe, lest the light of the gospel of the glory of Christ, who is the image of God, should shine on them."

Our first prayer must always be that Satan will be restricted and will not be able to exercise his "snatching power" over the Word of God being preached or taught. We must pray that Satan will be prohibited from blinding the eyes or deafening the ears of those who are in the presence of the gospel.

That the God of our Lord Jesus Christ, the Father of glory, may give to you the spirit of wisdom and revelation in the knowledge of Him, the eyes of your understanding being enlightened; that you may know what is the hope of His calling, what are the riches of the glory of His inheritance in the saints, and what is the exceeding greatness of His power toward us who believe, according to the working of His mighty power.

—Ephesians 1:17-19

∽ Give practical examples of things that you can do to help your children's eyes "be enlightened" to the gospel.

## ∞ The Blood ∞

Satan cannot cross the "blood line" that has been placed around those who accept Jesus Christ as their Savior. We bind Satan by declaring to him that we have been purchased by the shed blood of Christ Jesus. In so doing, we are declaring that we are the property of God, not the property of the devil. God has jurisdiction and power over our lives, not Satan.

But if we walk in the light as He is in the light, we have fellowship with one another, and the blood of Jesus Christ His Son cleanses us from all sin.

—1 John 1:7

☙ What does it mean to "walk in the light"? Give practical examples of how this is done.

☙ How can you help your family to keep walking in the light this week?

## ∞ The Name of Jesus ∞

When we confront Satan, we must do so in the name of the Lord Jesus Christ. It is in His name that we have authority over evil. Peter and John spoke to a lame man in the name of Jesus, and the man was healed. All who saw the man walking, leaping, and praising God were amazed, and the religious officials became so angry that they imprisoned Peter and

John. The next day the authorities interrogated them, and the Bible tells us, "Then Peter, filled with the Holy Spirit, said to them, 'Rulers of the people and elders of Israel: If we this day are judged for a good deed done to a helpless man, by what means he has been made well, let it be known to you all, and to all the people of Israel, that by the name of Jesus Christ of Nazareth, whom you crucified, whom God raised from the dead, by Him this man stands here before you whole'" (Acts 4:8–10).

There is great power in the name of Jesus! He has given us His name to use in bringing healing and deliverance to those who are oppressed, discouraged, and "sick" or "injured" in any area of their lives!

> And whatever you ask in My name, that I will do, that the Father may be glorified in the Son. If you ask anything in My name, I will do it.
>
> —John 14:13-14

☙ What does it mean to ask for something "in Jesus' name"?

☙ What do you think the Lord might want you to ask for on behalf of your family this week?

# A Verbal Declaration

Note that each of the "weapons" that Jesus has given us for binding Satan is a weapon that we exercise in the spirit realm *by our spoken words*. We are called to speak the name of Jesus, to speak about the blood of Christ, to speak the Word of God as we give our own personal testimony. We do not bind Satan by just thinking good thoughts or having the right attitude. Our faith is certainly at the foundation of our battle against Satan, but repeatedly we are told that our faith must be verbalized—it must be spoken aloud.

It is in speaking the name of Jesus that we make His presence and power real, ready, and available in any situation. To wish, hope, or even believe that Jesus will deliver us from Satan is not enough. We must declare it to be so!

> Therefore God also has highly exalted Him and given Him the name which is above every name, that at the name of Jesus every knee should bow, of those in heaven, and of those on earth, and of those under the earth, and that every tongue should confess that Jesus Christ is Lord, to the glory of God the Father.
>
> —Philippians 2:9-11

❧ Why does Paul speak of "knees" and "tongues" in this passage? What does this imply about our words and our deeds?

๛ How might confessing "that Jesus Christ is Lord" help a person to break out of bondage to sin?

---

## ๛ Today and Tomorrow ๛

*TODAY:* THROUGH THE NAME OF JESUS, MY FAMILY CAN FIND FREEDOM AND RESTORATION.

*TOMORROW:* THIS WEEK, I WILL PRAY THAT GOD WILL TEACH ME TO SPEAK THE NAME OF JESUS WITH BOLDNESS.

# LESSON 10

# Praying for and with Your Family

───────────  ⮞ **In This Lesson** ⮜  ───────────

*LEARNING:* HOW CAN I BEST PROTECT MY FAMILY?

*GROWING:* HOW SHOULD I PRAY FOR MY FAMILY?

Perhaps the most important thing that you can do to protect your family from evil is to intercede in prayer for them daily. We have a great example of this in Job. The book of Job begins by telling us that Job was a man who was "blameless and upright, and one who feared God and shunned evil" (1:1). He had seven sons and three daughters. We read in Job 1:5 that he rose "early in the morning" to "offer burnt offerings according to the number of them all. For Job said, 'It may be that my sons have sinned and cursed God in their hearts.' Thus Job did regularly."

Job's children were grown and lived in their own homes, yet he continued to make sacrifices for them every morning. In doing this, he was calling out to God on their behalf, requesting God's mercy on their lives. His prayer life for his family was a part of his very character; it was his nature to pray as a blameless and upright man who feared God and shunned evil.

We are called to follow in Job's example today. We are to live blameless and upright lives before our children and also to pray for our children daily, no matter how old they are or what circumstances they are in.

⮞ Do you have people who pray for you daily? Are there people that you pray for daily?

# A Hedge of Protection

God uses our prayers for others to establish a hedge of protection around them. This was Satan's lament when he sought to bring accusation against Job and to attack his life. He said, "Does Job fear God for nothing? Have You not made a hedge around him, around his household, and around all that he has on every side?" (Job 1:9–10). Job's life and his practice of intercession on behalf of his family were certainly major factors in God's creating a hedge of protection that Satan could not penetrate.

A "hedge" in Bible times was not a little row of bushes or shrubbery that might grow in a yard. It was considered to be a high wall or a fortress-like structure. Anything that was "hedged in" was fully protected from attack. The Bible tells us that God's hedge around us is generally established in one of two ways:

1. Through angels

2. Through righteous people

These are the foremost methods that God uses to provide protection for us.

## ⧉ Hedge of Angels ⧉

In Psalm 34:7 we read, "The angel of the LORD encamps all around those who fear Him, and delivers them." Elisha was a man who experienced an angelic hedge of angels. In 2 Kings 6 we read how the king of Syria was greatly troubled by Elisha, who kept telling the Israelite army his every move. He sought to kill Elisha, and discovered that he was residing in Dothan. 2 Kings 6:14–15, 17–18 tells us that the king of Syria:

> sent horses and chariots and a great army there, and they came by night and surrounded the city. And when the servant of the man of God [Elisha] arose early and went out, there was an army, surrounding the city with horses and chariots. And his servant said to him, "Alas, my master! What shall we do?" ... And Elisha prayed, and said, "LORD, I pray, open his eyes that he may see." Then the LORD opened the eyes of the young man, and he saw. And behold, the mountain was full of horses and chariots of fire all around Elisha. So when the Syrians came down to him, Elisha prayed to the LORD, and said, "Strike this people, I pray, with blindness." And He struck them with blindness according to the word of Elisha.

Elisha then led the blind army all the way to Samaria before their eyes were opened.

⧉ When have you witnessed God's miraculous protection of you or your family?

## ∞ Hedge Provided by a Righteous Person ∞

We find many references in the Bible to those who "stood in the gap" or "stood in the breach," people used by God to provide a defense for His righteous ones in the face of great danger. Psalm 106:23 describes Moses as one such person who provided a wall of protection: "Therefore He said that He would destroy them, had not Moses His chosen one stood before Him in the breach, to turn away His wrath, lest He destroy them."

Ezekiel 22:30–31 records these words of the Lord: "'I sought for a man among them who would make a wall, and stand in the gap before Me on behalf of the land, that I should not destroy it; but I found no one. Therefore I have poured out My indignation on them; I have consumed them with the fire of My wrath; and I have recompensed their deeds on their own heads,' says the Lord God."

Most of us do not experience this protective hedge for one simple reason: we do not pray with consistency and diligence for our families. What wondrous things we might see if we were to adopt a daily habit of praying diligently and fervently for those we love!

∞ When has someone "stood in the breach" on your behalf? When have you done that for someone else?

∞ What dangers are threatening your family at present?

# What Shall We Pray?

The Bible has a number of prayers that are appropriate for you to pray in behalf of your family. I recommend especially the prayer found in Colossians 1:9–14, which says:

> [We] do not cease to pray for you, and to ask that you may be filled with the knowledge of His will in all wisdom and spiritual understanding; that you may walk worthy of the Lord, fully pleasing Him, being fruitful in every good work and increasing in the knowledge of God; strengthened with all might, according to His glorious power, for all patience and longsuffering with joy; giving thanks to the Father who has qualified us to be partakers of the inheritance of the saints in the light. He has delivered us from the power of darkness and conveyed us into the kingdom of the Son of His love, in whom we have redemption through His blood, the forgiveness of sins.

Let's take a closer look at four specific things that Paul prays.

## 1. Wisdom and Spiritual Understanding About God's Will

Paul prays that the Colossians will be "filled with the knowledge of His will in all wisdom and spiritual understanding" (Col. 1:9). It is always appropriate to pray that we and our family will know God's will for our lives. God desires that we have His wisdom. Wisdom is highly practical—it is the knowledge of *how* to apply God's truths. God also desires that we have spiritual understanding, which is an understanding of how and why God does things the way He does them. Spiritual understanding is very close to discernment, which is the ability to see "behind the scenes" to the true motives for good or evil that are at work in any situation.

Ask God for wisdom and spiritual understanding. Ask Him to reveal His purposes in your life. Pray that your spouse and children might also know the reason for their creation, have greater wisdom in their daily decisions, and be able to discern what it is that God wants to do in their lives.

> If any of you lacks wisdom, let him ask of God, who gives to all liberally and without reproach, and it will be given to him. But let him ask in faith, with no doubting, for he who doubts is like a wave of the sea driven and tossed by the wind.
>
> James 1:5-6

🐾 Why does James tell us that God "gives to all liberally and without reproach"? How might a fear of reproach prevent you from praying for wisdom?

🐾 Why is it important to "ask in faith, with no doubting"? How might a lack of faith interfere with gaining wisdom?

## 2. Walking Worthy of the Lord

Paul prays that the Colossians may "walk worthy of the Lord, fully pleasing Him, being fruitful in every good work and increasing in the knowledge of God" (Colossians 1:10). The way to please God is stated here very clearly: be fruitful in ministry to others and develop an increasingly intimate relationship with God and His Word. That must be our prayer for ourselves, that we might discover new and more effective ways to help others, that we might have increasing insights into God's Word, and that we might have an ever-deepening relationship with the Lord. We are never amiss to pray this on behalf of our family members.

> I ... beseech you to walk worthy of the calling with which you were called, with all lowliness and gentleness, with longsuffering, bearing with one another in love.
>
> —Ephesians 4:1-2

∝ Give real-life examples of people who have lived with "lowliness and gentleness". What influence did they have on people around them?

∝ What is the "calling with which you were called"? How well are you fulfilling that calling lately?

### 3. Strengthened with All Might

Paul prays that the Colossians might be "strengthened with all might, according to His glorious power, for all patience and longsuffering with joy" (Colossians 1:11). The kind of strength that Paul seeks on their behalf is *enduring* power—the ability to survive times of persecution and to remain steadfast in faith. This kind of strength comes as we draw our strength from the Lord, relying on Him fully to help us when we cannot help ourselves. When we draw enduring power from the Lord, we also experience joy. We know that the Lord is helping us and that He is working on our behalf.

What gives us strength? Paul explains to the Ephesians that this kind of strength comes as we experience Christ's love—when we begin to understand how much God cares for us, and respond with His love welling up in our hearts. The person who is filled with love has *great* strength. What a wonderful thing to pray for your family, that each member will be filled to overflowing with God's love!

> [I pray] that He would grant you, according to the riches of His glory, to be strengthened with might through His Spirit in the inner man, that Christ may dwell in your hearts through faith; that you, being rooted and grounded in love, may be able to comprehend with all the saints what is the width and length and depth and height to know the love of Christ which passes knowledge; that you may be filled with all the fullness of God.
>
> —Ephesians 3:16-19

☙ Take a few minutes now to pray for your family, individually or as a group, using Paul's words as a starting-point. Put these verses into your own words.

## 4. Thanksgiving for Our Salvation

Paul concludes his prayer for the Colossians by "giving thanks to the Father who has qualified us to be partakers of the inheritance of the saints in the light" (Colossians 1:12). We, too, must offer praise and thanksgiving to God for our family members and, in particular, for their salvation. If members of your family are not saved, your number-one prayer for them should be that they will accept Christ. If your family members are saved, then your prayer should be one of ongoing thanksgiving as well as a prayer that they will continue to walk in the light of the Holy Spirit.

> I thank my God upon every remembrance of you, always in every prayer of mine making request for you all with joy, for your fellowship in the gospel from the first day until now, being confident of this very thing, that He who has begun a good work in you will complete it until the day of Jesus Christ.
>
> —Philippians 1:3-6

 How often do you thank God for each member of your family? Take a few minutes now to do so.

 Why does Paul say that God will "complete the good work *until* the day of Jesus Christ," rather than "*on*" that day? What does this imply about God's work in each member of your family?

119

## Praying with Your Family

You can use Paul's prayer and other prayers in the Bible as a part of your intercession for your family members, and you can also pray these prayers *with* your family members. Let your children know what you pray for them. Let them hear you pray. Invite their prayers for you in return, including a prayer that you will be the best parent possible. Prayer is something that every person can do for his family.

There is no excuse *not* to pray. God looks upon the intent of your heart as you pray; you don't need to be concerned about using "the right words." Neither should you be concerned that you aren't praying in precisely the right way. You are always praying for the right things if you are praying for the protection of God against evil, and requesting strength and wisdom so that your loved ones might withstand evil pressures. If you are praying out of love for your family and out of a desire to see God work in their lives, you are praying with the right motive.

Paul tells us to don the whole armor of God for spiritual battle, and he states that those dressed for spiritual warfare should be found "praying always with all prayer and supplication in the Spirit" (Ephesians 6:18). Pray for whatever it is that the Spirit prompts you to pray for your family members. Pray often. Pray about every situation, circumstance, relationship, and activity that involves your family members. Cover your family with prayer, and then trust God to cover them with His protection.

See then that you walk circumspectly, not as fools but as wise,
redeeming the time, because the days are evil.

—Ephesians 5:15-16

❧ What does it mean to "walk circumspectly"? Give practical
examples of this.

❧ How does a person "redeem the time"? In practical terms,
how does a parent do this for his family?

And this I pray, that your love may abound still more and more in knowledge and all discernment, that you may approve the things that are excellent, that you may be sincere and without offense till the day of Christ, being filled with the fruits of righteousness which are by Jesus Christ, to the glory and praise of God.

—Philippians 1:9-11

Put these verses into your own words, and begin to pray them every day this week for your family.

## Today and Tomorrow

*TODAY:* I CAN SET UP A "HEDGE" OF PROTECTION FOR MY FAMILY SIMPLY BY PRAYING FOR THEM DAILY.

*TOMORROW:* I WILL BEGIN TO PRAY EVERY DAY, BOTH *FOR* MY FAMILY AND *WITH* MY FAMILY.

## ❧ Notes and Prayer Requests: ❧

⌒∞⌒ **Notes and Prayer Requests:** ⌒∞⌒